DAVID BYRNE
SALLY RUANE

PAYING FOR THE WELFARE STATE IN THE 21ST CENTURY

Tax and spending in post-industrial societies

POLICY PRESS SHORTS INSIGHTS

First published in Great Britain in 2017 by

Policy Press
University of Bristol
1-9 Old Park Hill
Bristol
BS2 8BB
UK
t: +44 (0)117 954 5940
pp-info@bristol.ac.uk
www.policypress.co.uk

North America office:
Policy Press
c/o The University of Chicago Press
1427 East 60th Street
Chicago, IL 60637, USA
t: +1 773 702 7700
f: +1 773 702 9756
sales@press.uchicago.edu
www.press.uchicago.edu

British Library Cataloguing in Publication Data
A catalogue record for this book is available from the British Library.

Library of Congress Cataloging-in-Publication Data
A catalog record for this book has been requested.

ISBN 978-1-4473-3653-2 (paperback)
ISBN 978-1-4473-3655-6 (ePub)
ISBN 978-1-4473-3656-3 (Mobi)
ISBN 978-1-4473-3654-9 (ePDF)

Cover design by Policy Press
Front cover: image kindly supplied by Getty
Printed and bound in Great Britain by CMP, Poole
Policy Press uses environmentally responsible print partners

To our parents,
Betty and Tom who started with next to nothing and
raised a family under welfare capitalism
and Kathleen, who spent 14 years of her life working
for the Inland Revenue until the marriage bar and
motherhood knocked her out of it.

Contents

List of figures

List of tables

Acknowledgements

We have been much stimulated by our engagement with George Irvin, Howard Reed and Richard Murphy – our co-authors on the Compass Report *In Place of Cuts* and with Adrian Sinfield who has always been supportive and helpful. Any errors or omissions in this text are our responsibility alone.

Abbreviations and acronyms

AFL	American Federation of Labour
BREXIT	Exit of the UK from the European Union
CIO	Congress of Industrial Organizations (USA)
DWP	Department of Work and Pensions (UK)
ESA	Employment Support Allowance
FDR	Franklin Delano Roosevelt US President
GDP	gross domestic product
GHI	gross household income
GVA	gross value added
IEA	Institute of Economic Affairs
IFS	Institute for Fiscal Studies
IPPR	Institute for Public Policy Research
HMRC	Her Majesty's Revenue and Customs
JSA	Jobseekers' Allowance
IMF	International Monetary Fund
NAO	National Audit Office
NHS	National Health Service (UK)
NI	National Insurance
NICs	National Insurance Contributions
OECD	Organization for Economic Cooperation and Development
ONS	Office for National Statistics (UK)
PFI	Private Finance Initiative
PPE	politics, philosophy and economics

SDP	German Social Democratic Party
SNP	Scottish National Party
TUC	Trades Union Congress
UK	United Kingdom
USA	United States of America
VAT	Value Added Tax
WAS	Wealth and Assets Survey

Introduction:
Why understanding the tax system
is so important

If we want to understand the nature of societies like the UK, nation states formerly understood as 'advanced industrial countries' then we need to understand their tax systems and the way in which fundamental changes in the economic structure have profound implications for both tax systems and the wider social order. The direction of causation is *not* one way. How tax systems work matters for the economic structure itself. The assertion that understanding tax systems is important is not a new one. Schumpter, in a book pertinently entitled *The Fiscal Crisis of the Tax State*, stated:

> In some periods they [Fiscal Measures] explain practically all major events and in most periods they explain a great deal…But even greater than the causal is the symptomatic significance of fiscal history. The spirit of a people, its cultural level, its social structure, the deeds its policy may prepare…all this and more is written in fiscal history. He who knows how to listen to its message here discerns the thunder of world history more clearly than anywhere else. (1918, 101)

The term 'fiscal crisis' is central to our considerations. Our starting point is the explicitly Marxist account presented by O'Connor in *The*

Fiscal Crisis of the State (1973) and in his useful reconsideration in the preface to the 2002 reissued edition,[1] rather than Schumpeter, but the way in which two writers from such different political positions and at different times have associated the words 'fiscal' and 'crisis' tells us that there is something about taxation which is of crucial significance in periods when 'things cannot stay as they are'. If 'fiscal' is the covering term for taxation, 'crisis' is a word with its origins in early medicine. It described the point in the natural history of a case of a serious infection when the patient either got better because their immune system overcame the infection or died because the infection overcame their immune system. The idea of crisis works well in relation to the approaches which constitute the complexity frame of reference (Byrne, 1998; Byrne and Callaghan, 2013). Social complexity theory asserts that social systems at all levels are to be understood as complex, far from equilibric systems which are emergent. The state of these systems is a consequence of interactions among all components of the system and with other systems of significance, including, in particular, the ecological system. For the social system, the components are generally complex systems themselves at all levels including that of the individual and institutions. Complex social systems can and do remain relatively stable for longish periods of time but when they change they change in terms of kind rather than terms of degree. Historical sociology has focused exactly on such radical transformations. So, we can think of crisis as both a stage in the history of a social system and in terms of the causal configurations which drive such transformations. In Marxist terms this is usually expressed by the idea of contradiction.

Block (1981) summarised the notion of the drivers of fiscal crisis precisely in terms of contradiction. Drawing on O'Connor, he identified fiscal crisis as more than a gap between government expenditure and revenues – 'the deficit'. For Keynesians a deficit is not a problem. The proper function of government macro-economic policy in an economic downturn is to run a deficit in order to stimulate aggregate demand. To see a nation state's deficit as equivalent to a deficit for a household or a company is to commit a fallacy of composition. Fiscal crisis is not merely a deficit but rather a consequence of a fundamental contradiction in capitalism between the requirement on democratic states to achieve legitimacy by providing services to the population and at the same time the requirement that the state should not: 'raise taxes beyond levels that are seen as fair' (Block, 1981, 2) The crucial question is 'fair to whom or what?' Taxes are taken from the incomes of everybody but the taxes which are contradictory to capitalism are those taxes on income and property which redistribute from the owners of property to those dependent on wage labour or benefits in a way which does not facilitate capital accumulation. Westergaard (1978) outlined the limits to social reform in terms which recognised that in a capitalist social order taxation-based redistribution intended to provide services/benefits cannot challenge the fundamental right of the owners of property to receive an income return based on that ownership. Redistributive taxation can only go so far.

O'Connor showed that a part of state expenditure is functional for capital accumulation towards which a capitalist economy is necessarily oriented. Some of the revenue raised by taxation goes directly to subsidise capitalist corporations and more is spent covering costs which capitalist corporations would otherwise have to cover for themselves. Nonetheless a high proportion of state expenditure, funded from taxation,[2] goes on things which do no more or indeed no less for capitalism than maintain the legitimacy of the social order.

The systems of taxation and welfare in post-industrial industrial states were created in very large part to resolve the contradictions inherent in industrial capitalism – that is, capitalist societies in which the major form of capital accumulation was through the production of real commodities[3] and many economically active people were engaged in the production of those commodities with production being organised in factories and other similar workplaces with people selling their labour to the owners of capital. The characteristic system relating taxation and welfare in industrial societies was social insurance, introduced by Bismark in late nineteenth century Germany in order to see off the political threat of the German Social Democratic Party, which was a Marxist party dedicated to the replacement of capitalism by a radically different social order.

The expression of the contradiction in industrial capitalism which mattered most from the 1870s to the 1970s was the existence of an industrial proletariat, organised in trade unions and in political parties which had programmes for replacing capitalism with another kind of social order. Most Labour and Socialist Parties were not revolutionary in the sense of seriously considering revolutionary social change. They sought, through the gradual accretion of social and economic reforms and an ultimate transformation of quantity into quality, to convert capitalism into a socialist order. In practice, almost all abandoned such transformational reformism and instead saw their function as being to reform and moderate the abuses of the capitalist system and thereby serve the interests of people who sold their labour to earn a living.

In the early twenty-first century with the collapse of the Soviet System in Europe and the emergence of Communist China into the world's largest industrial capitalist state under a Communist Party government, the notion that capitalism ever felt seriously threatened by a socialist alternative may seem strange, although one implication of the argument of this book is that such a time is rather likely to come again. During the Second World War, Beveridge – a UK Liberal and not socialist – (whose 1942 Report was foundational to post-Second World War welfare capitalism), actually asserted that if capitalism could not provide full employment and the welfare arrangements that flowed from it, then capitalism would have to be replaced by something else.[4]

The transition to post-industrialism has not only weakened the social base of socialist and Labour parties across the formerly industrial world. At its most extreme in the United Kingdom a Labour Party, explicitly founded to use parliamentary means to ensure that Trade Unions could function effectively, during its 13-year period of office from 1997 to 2010 did virtually nothing to repeal legislation introduced by the Thatcher government which rendered real trade union action extremely difficult. Labour and socialist parties bought in to the notion that capital was in charge and the best they could do was to work with it. The causal processes here were absolutely recursive. Deindustrialisation weakened the organised working class which weakened the social base of left parties. The failure of left parties to develop a coherent alternative programme for post-industrial capitalism weakened the very social base from which such parties drew their support. It was exactly a vicious circle. One aspect of these changes which has massive implications for the tax bases of post-industrial capitalist societies was the active encouragement by 'left' governments, particularly New Labour in the UK, of privatisation of previously publicly delivered services in kind, yet another policy which directly weakened their own social base.

Social Insurance systems in industrial capitalism were horizontal transfers across risks of unemployment and sickness in working life and across generations through the funding of pensions. The transfers were horizontal because the tax was levied on workers – employers' contributions are recognised by all labour economists to be part of the wage bill, not a tax on employers – and the benefits went to workers and retired workers. Entitlements were based on contributory record without any means testing. Social insurance was insurance, but even in its purest forms it was also a tax since contributions were mandatory. Insurance schemes were generally supplemented by some form of means tested social assistance provision for those who for one reason or another were not entitled to benefits or who had exhausted that entitlement. During the great depression of the 1930s the number of insured workers who had exhausted their unemployment insurance entitlements was a major issue in British politics and the social assistance support of such workers was transferred from local authorities to the central state.[5]

During what regulation theory (see Byrne, 2005 for a discussion of this school)[6] describes as the Keynesian mode of regulation and Hobsbawm (1995) called 'The Golden Years' – the third quarter of the twentieth century, full employment across industrial capitalism meant that the fiscal base of social insurance systems and even of systems outside social insurance such as the UK's National Health Service[7] was generally sound. General taxation in industrial capitalist democracies was used to fund redistribution of income in cash and kind. The ability of states to control flows of capital and income across their borders remained considerable and although there was a good deal of tax evasion and even more tax avoidance, neither of these were at a level as to threaten the fiscal stability of nation states. In consequence in the UK from 1945 to the end of the 1970s, social inequality was at its lowest level ever.

The combination of deindustrialisation and globalisation has changed all this. The tax systems which worked for industrial welfare capitalism, no longer work in post-industrial capitalism because the terms and conditions and nature of work for many in post-industrial capitalism are all radically different from those of the industrial era. There are two factors in this, both covered well for the UK in Beatty and Fothergill (2016). Deindustrialisation has imposed a massive dependency burden on public revenues with many non-workers maintained on Employment Support Allowance (ESA) payable to those who have limiting capacities in relation to work. Together with associated means tested housing and other benefits Beatty and Fothergill estimate this as costing at least £30 billion. And there are the Speenhamland supplements to low wages which are now the core of the UK welfare system. Consequently, there is the massive loss in tax revenues since such low paid or wageless workers pay less in tax than they receive in benefits in contrast to the net tax contribution of fully employed relatively well-paid workers in the industrial era.[8]

Let us revisit the implications of using a complexity frame of reference in addressing the issues posed for tax systems by deindustrialisation. We do not see the causal pattern as being simply one in which deindustrialisation/globalisation has caused changes in tax systems. Certainly, the way in which these changes weakened the social and institutional base of political parties of the left and centre left, has been a crucial factor in changing the nature of governance in general and tax systems in particular. However, changes in tax systems have reinforced the dominance of financial capital over industrial capital, further weakening the power base of the industrial working class. Developments in tax and benefits, and particularly the reinvention of Speenhamland type benefits, have reinforced the transformation of work towards 'flexible employment' – itself an important driver of the profound changes associated with the post-industrial transformation.

There has been positive feedback in the system. Changes in tax systems, particularly the weak enforcement of collection of taxes from global corporations and the super-rich, have reinforced the drive towards financialisation of previously industrial economies. All this together has contributed towards ever greater inequality.

The purpose of this book is to outline the character of these changes in relation to a framework which draws on a Marxist understanding of the contradictions between tax revenue funded services in welfare capitalism and the character of capitalism in a post-industrial era in the 'west'. We will deploy the understanding of the fiscal crisis developed by O'Connor drawing also on his clear analytical discussion of the nature of crisis in general. Not only will we attempt to update his analyses in relation to the character of post-industrial capitalism, we will do so in a contemporary context where what in Chapter Three we will identify after Aalbers (2016) as a crisis in the quaternary (financial) circuit of accumulation, has thrown the whole edifice of welfare capitalism into question. We are in an era of 'austerity' in which budgetary deficits, caused by the transfer of the costs of financial failure from banks and related corporate entities to the public exchequer, are used to justify downsizing the whole welfare capitalist state.

We are not going to confine ourselves to analysis and description but will make suggestions as to how a government of any kind of left persuasion might seek to address these issues. Our approach is radical and grounded not in the technicalities of economistic approaches which take the present state of capitalist relations for granted and do not grasp the seriousness of the crisis confronting the post-industrial capitalist social order. Typical of these was the Mirrlees Review (Mirrlees et al, 2011). This contains useful information but the fundamental underlying assumptions, especially the reliance on the equilibric conceptions which inform contemporary neoclassical economics, render it useless in understanding and dealing with the situation which confronts us today. We agree with one thing which Mirrlees et al said (Adam et al, 2010; Mirrlees et al, 2011). Tax must be understood as a system and taxes taken together in terms of their effects rather than regarded as discrete separate entities. For us, however, tax must be understood as a complex system in intersection with all sorts of other systems, most obviously in relation to cash benefit systems but also with all the systems which constitute the economic foundation of our contemporary social order. It is useful here to contrast the very limited and conventional approach to taxation represented by Mirrlees et al (2011) with the radical class analysis presented by O'Connor:

> The primary task we have set ourselves is to identify reforms that would make the tax system more efficient, while raising roughly the same amount of revenue as the current system and while redistributing resources to those with high needs or low incomes to roughly the same degree. (Mirrlees et al, 2011, 2)

> [T]ax systems are simply particular forms of class systems. (O'Connor 1973; 2002, 206)

We are with O'Connor and what follows here is a class analysis of tax systems in post-industrial industrial capitalism, an analysis attempted exactly during a period of crisis.

This book is organised as follows. Chapter One is our first engagement with the fiscal crisis in post-industrial capitalism with a focus on the functions of welfare and taxation 'after industry'. Here O'Connor's discussion of the fiscal crisis of the state will be reviewed in relation to the nature of taxation in post-industrial capitalism. The chapter will begin with an outline of O'Connor's arguments as they were originally developed in relation to capitalism as an industrial system in the era of developed welfare states. It will then outline the fundamental transformation from an industrial to post-industrial capitalism in terms of the changing composition of the economic base in industrial and now post-industrial societies.

Chapter Two will develop our discussion of the fiscal crisis in post-industrial capitalism with a focus on the nature and scope of taxation. It begins with a historical discussion of the forms of taxation – of incomes through income tax and social insurance, of consumption through indirect taxes, of private real property through land taxes, and of profits through corporation taxes. The contemporary status of these elements will be considered with some comparisons made between the UK, Scandinavia, Germany, France and the USA. The issues which arise from the ability of both corporations and very high income individuals/households to avoid national tax through transnational transfers will be examined. The chapter will conclude with a discussion of the issues posed by such transfers and the character of tax systems overall for the funding of welfare states. Here we will begin our consideration of the redistributive impact of tax systems and the relation of tax systems to social inequality which will be developed in detail in Chapter Four.

Chapter Three will engage with issues of debt, austerity and welfare in post-industrial capitalism. This chapter will set 'paying for welfare' in relation to the political and economic context of 'after the crash'. It will draw on Streeck's discussion of the macro politics of public debt in what continues to be (having strangely not died – Crouch, 2011) the neoliberal dominance of political and economic debate among political elites. Not only are these societies post-industrial. They are also in Crouch's terms 'post-democratic', that is, they have all the institutional forms of democracy but with parties generally endorsing a 'business' rationale with very little real ideological difference in formal politics. There will also be a consideration of the role of the media and the way in which the dominant trend in media presentation has represented the causes of the current crisis and the scope for remedies to it. This will draw on and engage critically with the important arguments advanced by Blyth in his magisterial *Austerity: The History of a Dangerous Idea* (2013a). We agree wholly with Blyth's account of the way austerity has been sold as a cultural and political imperative, as a constituent of what Edward Thompson called Experience II – the understanding of the social order created by all the pressures brought to bear on people's mindsets by the pressures of the media and what we might call the ideological state apparatuses – what 'they' tell us things are like. When we engage with Thompson's Experience I – our understandings as shaped by lived experience in relation to the character of the capitalist social order – which in his lovely phrase 'walks in the door without knocking' (1981), and do so in a period of not only fiscal but basal crisis, then perhaps the kind of Keynesian alternative proposed by Blyth will not work again. We will begin this engagement in Chapter Three but continue it in the conclusion.

Chapter Four will continue our examination of the relationship between tax systems and inequality in post-industrial capitalism. There is a substantial literature on economic inequality arising from variations in incomes and benefits but very little on the contribution of taxation and of public spending on services (rather than benefits) to the extent and patterning of inequality. This chapter will examine the incidence of personal taxation upon households and the shifts in this from the 1970s to the present day, using official data and will examine evidence of the distribution of public spending by household income. The inextricable link between the falling share of national income enjoyed by most workers and the rising fortunes of the top 1 per cent will be examined, along with aspects of the tax system which reinforce those divergent experiences. Given the significance of tax avoidance by high income households the real extent of inequality is considerably greater than that indicated in the data series which are used to calculate Gini coefficients and other measures of the extent of inequality across a society. Here we will try to see how taxes as a whole system work primarily using the UK as an example but also drawing on illustrative material from other post-industrial states.

Chapter Five will explore the politics of tax and welfare in twenty-first century post-industrial capitalism. Essentially this is a crisis of social democracy although perhaps not so much a crisis of labourism, given that the central principle of labourism – the defence of the ability of workers to organise and defend themselves against exploitation at work – had already been abandoned by parties which still retain the name Labour. Social Democratic/'Labour' parties no longer even pretend to present a radical alternative to capitalist socialist relations. They shifted from this position to becoming essentially defenders of the Keynes/ Beveridge style of welfare capitalism by the 1960s, although in a post-industrial context they can no longer even do that. Instead they present themselves as moderators of the inevitable logic of neoliberalism and consequent 'austerity'. It will be bad, they say, but we will make it not quite so bad. The chapter will look at the issues as they emerge generally across the heartlands of social democracy.

Much useful material about tax and spending became available around the Scottish independence referendum and the subsequent Devo Max negotiations. Relating this to the subsequent course of Scottish politics allows us to explore the relationships between technical aspects of taxation and the political arguments and possibilities as these are presented to electorates. Scotland serves as a case study for the economic and political implications of the new fiscal crisis of the post-industrial state. Of particular political significance has been the ability of the Scottish Nationalist Party (SNP) to position itself to the left of UK Labour and effectively wipe out Labour as a UK national political force in Scotland. It has done this despite doing very little in relation to its quite real devolved taxation powers as the governing party in Scotland. These issues have become even clearer in the aftermath of BREXIT and Scotland's -vote to remain within the European Union. Here we have a well-documented illustration of the fiscal basis of the issues identified by Unger when he described the modern centre-left as seeming 'content to appear on the stage of contemporary history as humanisers of the inevitable'. (2015) The question is absolutely: is there no alternative? The Scottish case will be used to present the problems.

In the conclusion, the arguments will be drawn together. Using the language of the complexity frame of reference, we will return to the implications of understanding the present state of post-industrial industrial societies as being at a transition point in a crisis. The current trajectory of what was 'welfare capitalism' is towards gross inequality and 'post welfare'. What taxation policies could be used to create a social order that retains the essentials of the welfare state in a post-industrial social order? What political shifts are required to make them happen? Here we will make some preliminary suggestions and attempt to identify what institutional forms might seek in order to achieve such a shift in the trajectories of our sort of societies. It will be very much a case of optimism of the will triumphing over pessimism of the intellect but we are heartened by remembering Edward Thompson's assertion that in times of crisis Experience I – the reality of everyday life as opposed to Experience II – everything which the media and dominant culture presents to people – breaks through and another world does become possible.

Notes

[1] All page references to O'Connor in this book are to the 2009 edition.

[2] Although central banks do create money to fund state expenditures, most recently in the form of massive 'quantitative easing' to support a financial services sector which might otherwise have collapsed taking the whole economic system with it, it is taxation which pays for state's activities most generally.

[3] 'Real' here does not just mean material goods. Any commodity which provides a use is real, so, for example, computer programmes as sets of electrons are real commodities.

[4] In *Full Employment in a Free Society* (1944).

[5] There were two drivers for this. First, those areas with the greatest need had the least resources to meet that need. Second, some Labour controlled authorities were 'too generous' and/or had used local social assistance to support workers engaged in industrial disputes.

[6] A major weakness of regulation theory was insufficient attention to the importance of taxation.

[7] Although this has always been in part funded by a subvention from social insurance payments but with no requirement for a contribution record as a basis for entitlement to treatment.

[8] The agency form of employment where workers are not employees of the actual enterprise for which they work but of an agency which contracts to deliver them to that enterprise, is associated not only with low wages for the workers but with massive and systematic tax evasion. Phony offshore companies are established as beneficial owners of the agencies and these go into liquidation leaving unpaid not only taxes levied on them – corporation tax, but also the taxes collected by them – income tax and national insurance.

ONE

Fiscal crisis in post-industrial capitalism

O'Connor's (1973) schemata of the purposes of public expenditure remains a classic and persuasive new Marxist analysis of just what the capitalist state is doing when it spends money. The typology has stood the test of time and remains just as applicable today as it did more than 40 years ago. However, the context in which O'Connor framed it has changed profoundly, as he himself recognised in his thoughtful (2002) reflection in his foreword to the Transaction Publishers (2002) new edition. In this chapter we want to lay out in detail O'Connor's framework for understanding public expenditure, but first it is necessary to locate his original framing in relation to his description of the character of capitalism, and in particular as he noted United States capitalism at the time he was writing.[1] Wherever O'Connor used the word 'capitalism' we would add the adjective 'industrial'. Of course, the world continues to include enormous industrial capitalist societies but, as O'Connor recognised in 2002, globalisation had relocated much industrial production to China and the Global South and all the trends he identified then have accelerated since. The societies, which the authors were taught in our undergraduate years to identify as 'advanced industrial', are now post-industrial and that transformation has the most profound significance for any coherent understanding of the relationships among taxation, public expenditure, politics and the general social order. So, in this chapter we will begin by outlining O'Connor's description of the character of industrial capitalism. Then we will lay out in detail his analytical typology of the purposes of public expenditure. Next we will outline the differences between the industrial capitalism described by O'Connor and contemporary post-industrial capitalism. The chapter will conclude with a consideration of the implications of the post-industrial transformation for taxation, public expenditure and the form and character of welfare states.

Industrial capitalism: monopoly, competitive and state sectors[2]

For O'Connor, production in industrial capitalism took place in three sectors of the economy:

- The monopoly sector with large firms and large production units where:

  the growth of production depends less on growth of employment than on increases in physical capital per worker and technical progress. (2002, 15)

  This sector was unionised with workers seeking higher wages which could be paid without reduction in profits because this sector could pass on wage costs as higher prices. O'Connor perhaps pays insufficient attention to the role of increased productivity based on technical innovation and changing work practices as a basis for higher wages without increases in unit costs. In an era of expanding consumption this kind of change did not necessarily result in job loss although it always had the potential to replace living with dead labour, workers with capital goods. The monopoly sector was essentially industrial with firms located in manufacturing, large-scale extractive industries, major transport and energy and telecommunications sectors.
- The competitive sector with small firm and small production units. Here:

the physical capital-to-labour ratio and output per worker, or productivity, are low, and growth in production depends less on physical capital and technical progress than on growth of employment. (2002 13)

This sector dominated services and distribution although O'Connor included some manufacturing, including clothing, in the sector. It was typically non-unionised with relatively low wages. O'Connor does not comment on the gender composition of the workforce, but much of it was female.

- The state sector which, for O'Connor, included both production delivered by workers directly employed by the state in its various forms and production by private sector firms with contracts with the state.

    ... production in both categories of state industries depends on the state's budgetary priorities and its ability to mobilize tax revenues. Taxpayers bear costs in both sets of activities (including state contractors' profits), except for those wholly or partly organized on benefit principle [that is, charges are made for the services]. (2002, 17)

O'Connor did not originally distinguish between state production of a non-valorised form that is, work by directly state employed workers, and work done for the state on a for-profit basis, although he later addressed this issue in relation to the very important trend towards privatisation of formerly directly provided state services.

The only modification which would have been required in O'Connor's account in order to generalise it beyond the USA and across advanced industrial capitalist societies (one which he himself explicitly noted), was to take account of the significance, particularly in western Europe, of nationalised industries in primary production, manufacturing and energy provision. These produced commodities for sale but were part of the state although usually managed outwith the political process and direct political control. The USA had a postal service of this form but not much else. These were not in general funded by taxation and although their borrowing usually formed part of state capital budgets, they had a different character from directly or indirectly provided services delivered free of charge.

The United Kingdom (UK) of the early 1970s was a typical example of a western European advanced industrial society. The 1971 census counted nearly 24 million in the workforce. The industrial sectors of mining and manufacturing employed 36.2 per cent of this workforce to which we might add the 7.1 per cent employed in construction and the 8.2 per cent employed in utilities and transport. So more than half the workforce was employed in the industrial sector, broadly defined. Nearly 40 per cent were employed in services.

There are other accounts of the nature of the period O'Connor was describing which are complementary to his but also identify the particular character of Hobsbawm's (1995) 'golden years'. One of the most useful is regulation theory's account of 'the Keynesian mode of regulation'. The general framework of regulation theory is built around a distinction between 'the regime of accumulation' – that is the general pattern of organisation of the processes of capitalist production towards the end of accumulation, and 'the mode of regulation', which term covers the complex of institutions and normative structures which surround and govern the processes of capitalist reproduction both of labour power and of the social structure more generally. In this framework the term 'the Keynesian mode of regulation' refers to the complex of economic and social policy interventions which covered both the kind of welfare state typified by that developed on Beveridge's principles in the UK after 1945 and the tuning of economic policy both towards the facilitation of capital accumulation and the maintenance of full employment with an emphasis on smoothing out cyclical recessionary trends through the maintenance of overall aggregate demand. The term 'Fordism' is used both to describe a particular form of industrial production – mass production through a highly systematised division of labour typified by the assembly line – and a form of labour/capital relation in which workers were paid relatively well and were therefore able to afford the kind of products they made. In Marxist terms this involved a shift, already underway for skilled workers since the mid-nineteenth century, from the extraction of absolute surplus value based on increased labour time to relative surplus value based on increased labour productivity.

In this scenario welfare state expenditures, and in particular relatively high levels of wage substitution incomes for the unemployed in times of recession, were important Keynesian tools directed towards the maintenance of aggregate demand. High levels of national insurance-style unemployment benefits mattered but they were set in a context of the maintenance of high employment levels so that the funding of such schemes was assured in good times in a way which could both fund payments in bad times and make it less likely in consequence that bad times became worse and lasted longer. In a recession governments should be fully prepared to run a fiscal deficit to fund wage substitution benefits as well as spending on appropriate infra-structure development.

If we look at the tax structure of the UK at this time using OECD historical records[3] we see an interesting pattern. In 1965 the major sources of tax revenue were taxes on the incomes, profits and capital gains of individuals at 33 per cent and total indirect taxes at 33 per cent. National insurance raised 15.4 per cent of revenue and property taxes raised 14.5 per cent. Taxes on the profits of corporations raised 4.4 per cent of revenue. In the early 1970s the basic rate of income tax was 30 per cent with higher rates going up to 75 per cent in steps. There was an additional surcharge of 15 per cent on investment income making the top rate for that 90 per cent. The national insurance contribution was 5.5 per cent up to the upper limit. This means that the usual rate of tax for many but not all working (that is, working for wages or salaries) tax payers was 35.5 per cent although the earnings-related contribution element of national insurance was then linked to an entitlement to earnings related benefits.

National insurance as a tax/benefits system was the characteristic tax/cash benefit relation of an industrial society and in many countries this also was the basis of health entitlements. The general principle of insurance related benefits for workers had been devised in Bismarkian Germany in the late nineteenth century as a method of circumventing the threat of a socialist alternative to capitalism consequent on the emergence of avowedly socialist parties in societies which were moving towards mass democracy. This was widely imitated, for example in the Liberal Reforms of the immediate pre-First World War period in the UK. The essence of the system was that contributions would be collected from both workers and employers. In return for these contributions workers had defined entitlements, originally to wage substitution payments when unemployed or too sick to work but with a very important extension of this to pensions in old age in the UK beginning in the interwar years and consolidated with the establishment by the Labour government of the post-1945 welfare state. Even in the UK where the levels of benefit paid were low by western European standards, entitlements were real. For example, in 1979 the national insurance unemployment benefit for a fully entitled worker lasted for 12 months and was paid at a basic rate equal to 20 per cent of average earnings with additional elements for dependents. The almost complete breaking of any real link in the UK between national insurance payments and benefit entitlements for those of working age is one of the key tax/benefit changes consequent on the post-industrial transformation.[4] The link is more or less retained for old age pensions although not in terms of the relative to wages value of the benefit.

The purposes of public expenditure

The core of *The Fiscal Crisis of the State* is O'Connor's specification of the purposes of public expenditure. This typology is not a typology of specific budget headings, of specific forms of actual expenditure. Rather it is a description of the purposes which elements of any budget serve in relation to the maintenance of the integrity of the capitalist system of production. The explanation is functionalist but there is nothing wrong with that. Sometime we need to pay attention the role activities play in the maintenance of the form of the social system as a whole.

O'Connor's starting point is that the state has to fulfil two basic and often mutually contradictory functions:

- It has to ensure that social and economic arrangements are such that capital accumulation can happen and happen in a way which works best for capitalists.
- It has to maintain social harmony given that there is a fundamental conflict between capitalists who own the means of production and those who work for capital which centres around the necessity for capital and capitalists to exploit workers, that is, take from the workers some of the value of their production – surplus value in Marxist terms. This necessarily requires that through taxation the state returns some of the surplus value removed by exploitation to workers in the form of both cash and services in kind. This return can be regarded as a social wage although that term was coined by Italian autonomists after O'Connor laid out his schema.

So, state expenditures have to be organised in a way which facilitates these functions and attempts to some degree to resolve the conflict between them.

There are for O'Connor two basic purposes of state expenditure. The first is *social capital* – expenditure which facilitates the accumulation of capital itself. This in turn can be subdivided into *social investment* – expenditures which increase the productivity of a given amount of labour power, and *social consumption* – expenditures which lower the reproduction costs of labour power. We can see that, for example, health and education expenditures serve both purposes. A healthy and well-educated workforce is in principle more productive. At the same time if the state provides free healthcare and education then workers do not have to pay for them from wages nor do employers have to provide them as part of a wage package so there is less pressure on wage costs. The other purpose of social expenditure concerned with the legitimation of the social order, O'Connor called *social expenses*. Expenditure here is not just on legitimation, although in capitalist democracies that is the main function. Social expenses include expenditure on the coercive elements of the state – policing, incarceration and so on. Both health and education expenditures have a social expenses element in them. In contemporary post-industrial capitalist societies the great bulk of health expenditure is spent on old people past the working age who will not usually work again. Indeed, a great deal of this is spent in the last year of people's lives. This does not facilitate accumulation but the provision of decent healthcare in old age is a great justifier of social arrangements. Education doesn't just train up workers in work related skills: to use Althusser's term, education systems are ideological state apparatuses which also assert the legitimacy of an existing social order.

The fiscal crisis arises because:

> although the state has socialized more and more capital costs, the social surplus (including profits) continues to be appropriated privately. The socialisation of costs and the private appropriation of profits creates a fiscal crisis, or 'structural gap' between state revenues and state expenditures. The result is a tendency for state expenditures to increase more rapidly than the means of funding them. While the accumulation of social capital indirectly increases total production and society's surplus and this in principle appears to underwrite the expansion of social expenses, large monopoly capital corporations and unions strongly resist the appropriation of this surplus for new social capital expense outlays. (O'Connor, 2002, 9)

The reference to unions is somewhat US specific given the element of socialist principles informing western European unions.[5] It is even more specific in time given the legislatively enforced weakness of trade unions, especially in the UK and US. We should add, as O'Connor himself does, that it is not only corporations which resist taxation but also of course the very wealthy individuals, that is, the owners of the means of production, who benefit from exploitation.

Post-industrial capitalism: a profile

The United Kingdom was the world's first industrial capitalist society and, along with West Germany, was at the peak of its industrialisation in the 1960s, one of the two societies which had the highest proportion of its working-age population ever engaged in industrial employment. Although there had been significant job loss in the post-war years in some key industrial sectors, notably coal mining and traditional textiles, the development of new consumer goods and other light industries and the massive growth in female industrial employment in these sectors, meant that the UK's peak of industrialism was at that time.

The most recent UK census was 2011 and then the proportion of the workforce in England and Wales engaged in manufacturing was just 9 per cent. In the most broadly defined definition of industrial jobs – that is mining (very little), manufacturing, utilities, construction and transport, the total proportion of the workforce so engaged was 23.0 per cent. This was exceeded by the proportion engaged in state, health, education and related 'state sector' locations at 28 per cent with the great bulk of the remaining 50 per cent working in the private services sector. If we look at Scotland, historically one of the most industrial parts of the UK, then in 2011 just 8 per cent of the workforce were in manufacturing jobs with 27 per cent in industrial jobs broadly defined. Scotland was heavily dependent on welfare state-type employment in the 'state sector' with 30 per cent of employment being in this category. In 1981 when deindustrialisation was already underway Scotland had 24 per cent of its workforce in manufacturing with 43 per cent in industrial jobs broadly defined.

Changes in the character of employment are not simply a matter of sector of employment. There have also been profound changes in the gender composition of the workforce and in the balance among full-time employment, part-time employment and self-employment. In 1981 for Great Britain out of a total workforce of some 23 million, 59 per cent were male and 41 per cent were female; 9 per cent were self-employed. Part time employment was low for men but 39 per cent of women were employed part time. In 2011, with a workforce total of nearly 29 million, the gender composition for England and Wales was now 53 per cent male and 47 per cent female; 8 per cent of males and 33 per cent of females were part-time employees. The self-employed now constituted 14 per cent of the workforce. Scotland had a workforce of 2.7 million with 52 per cent males and 48 per cent females; 12 per cent of Scottish economically active males were part-time employees and 86 per cent full-time employees. For females, the figure was 37 per cent part-time employees and 49 per cent full-time employees; 15 per cent of economically active adults were self-employed.

Increases in labour productivity mean that a decline in numbers employed in a sector does not simply map on to a decline in the relative importance of production in that sector to the economy as a whole. Manufacturing value added has held up better than manufacturing employment, but even here there has been a massive relative decline. So, in 1991 manufacturing provided 21 per cent of the UK's value added but by 2008 this had declined to 12 per cent. Manufacturing was the most important provider of value added in 1991 but by 2008 it had been exceeded by real estate, renting and business activities at 24 per cent compared with 16 per cent in 1991 and almost matched by the wholesale and retail trade at 11 per cent, which was the same as in 1991.

The post-industrial era is characterised not just by these massive changes in the sectoral location of employment and value added, but also by fundamental changes in the character of the employment relation. The key policy term which describes this transformation is 'flexible labour market'. By this is meant a labour market in which the institutional safeguards protecting not only job security but also terms and conditions of employment, are systematically removed to the advantage of employers and capital and the disadvantage of workers. First and foremost, this takes the form of legislation which reduces the effective power of trade unions in conducting industrial disputes. This is not about smashing the unions – by which is meant the elimination of unions from the industrial scene, although this legislation has made it very difficult for unions to penetrate major new areas of employment, including privately provided, but state funded areas like social care. Actually, weak unions are useful social regulator since they can act to limit the spontaneous resistance of exploited workers. Second, there has been the generalisation of new forms of labour contract typified by 'zero-hours' in which the worker is available to the employer solely in relation to the employer's need for that labour. Related and overlapping with zero-hours is the massive growth in agency employment where the worker is not employed directly by the enterprise which directly benefits from that work but at one or more – often several – removes by an agency which exists to provide labour on this basis.

Agency work exists across the whole production spectrum from agricultural workers employed by gang masters but working on contract on farms, to cleaners in the offices of Her Majesty's Revenue and Customs – the UK's tax agency which is also tasked with enforcing minimum wage legislation – to call centre workers handing contact with a range of state agencies including much of local government and the 'Next Steps' agencies which deliver key national services, including social insurance benefits. In the UK, the only domestic policy initiative which moves against flexibility is a legally enforceable minimum wage. However, this is set below a living wage and enforcement is very weak. Some elements of the European Social Chapter offer some protections in terms of employment rights and limits on hours of work. However, these countervailing elements have done little to redress the negative aspects of flexibility, particularly for younger workers as entrants into the labour market without the protection of existing job rights.

Figures produced in 2016 by the UK Office for National Statistics (Chandler, 2016) show that just over 800,000 employees – 2.5 per cent of the workforce – regarded themselves as being on zero-hours contracts. Employers reported that they employed some 1.7 million people on contracts which did not offer guaranteed hours. The true total figure of zero-hours workers will be somewhere between these two. The Labour Force Survey figures (Chandler, 2016) showed that the zero-hours workers were differentially young – 38 per cent aged from 16 to 24 compared with 12 per cent in employment not on zero-hours in this age group, and often in full-time education – 23 per cent compared with 3 per cent normally employed. Those aged 21 to 24 are currently (April 2017) entitled only to a lower national minimum wage of £7.05 per hour and those aged 18 to 20 to a wage of £5.60 compared with the over-25 rate of £7.50 so the young are both cheap and flexible as labour. ONS Labour Force survey data indicated that there were some 320,000 agency workers in the UK in 2012 whereas employers' data suggests (Experian, 2010) that there are some 1.3 million 'temps'. The true figure again will lie somewhere between these two although almost certainly there are in excess of 1 million workers on this kind of contract. Of course, many agency workers are on zero-hours contracts so there will be overlap between the two categories.

Standing (2011) has coined the term 'precariat' to refer to people who lack a secure connection with the labour market. The term is, quite properly, fuzzy in relation to specification but plainly those who are on zero-hours contracts or insecure agency terms of employment will form part of this group. An important characteristic of the precariat is either or both of underemployment or portmanteau employment. That is people are not working enough hours to support themselves from labour income alone or obliged to have multiple different jobs in order to get by, or not, as the case may be. Chandler (2016) notes that 37 per cent of workers on zero-hours contracts wanted more work compared with 10 per cent of those not so employed. In 2015 the UK Labour Force Survey estimated that there were 1.16 million workers with at least a second job. Not all those with multiple jobs will have a first job which is in some way precarious, but many will. In addition, there are many who work for no remuneration including unpaid interns and those working as a condition of benefit receipt.

One very interesting shift in the UK since the financial crash is that the UK's total public sector employment has declined from 21 per cent of the labour force in March 2011 to 17 per cent in March 2016. Much of this is due to reclassification with the Royal Mail and partly denationalised Lloyds Bank being transferred from the public to private sectors, but also all universities and FE colleges are now counted as private sector with an increasing degree of private sector employment in the English but not Welsh and Scottish National Health Services and with ongoing privatisation in local authority services, particularly in the important area of domiciliary social care. Direct public sector employment is no necessary protection in relation to employment remuneration and conditions. Across England most classroom assistants in schools are now not being paid in the school holidays, whereas before they were paid on a yearly basis.

One of the best descriptions of this whole process and its consequences is provided by Nelson:

> postindustrial capitalism does not involve any shift in the fundamental process of capitalism as reflected in the competitive search for economic advantage or political dominance...What this new and blended form of capitalism does, however, is produce a transformation, a qualitative and discontinuous shift in class structure. That is, the contrast of past and present is indicated not merely by the blended form capitalism assumes but also by its influence on inequality. In previous time, economic development fed social development by diminishing inequality: today economic development escalates inequality. (1995, 14)

That prescient statement was written well before the financial crash when post-industrial capitalism seemed to be up and running well, although as Crouch (2000) has noted, this success was driven in large part by a 'privatised Keynesianism' – by a massive increase in personal and household debt by consumers in relation to both the purchase of consumer goods produced in the new industrial nations and the increasing costs of housing with massive inflation in house prices and rents, particularly in the English-speaking countries. The latter element was of course one of the factors leading to the sub-prime mortgages problems which triggered the liquidity and asset-based financial crash.

The ideological cover and colour of the whole process of system transformation – the phase shift in complexity theory terms – from industrial to post-industrial capitalism has been provided by neoliberalism. For Crouch neoliberalism's:

> one dominant theme [is] that free markets in which individuals maximize their material interests provide the best means for satisfying human aspirations, and that markets are in particular to

be preferred to the state and politics, which are at best inefficient and at worst threats to freedom. (2011, vii)

Neoliberalism as a political doctrine is closely associated with and supported by what has been until very recently the dominant neoclassical school in contemporary academic economic theory. This has continued a tradition of abstraction hiding its simplistic and unscientific (because devoid of empirical referent) assertions behind, as Joan Robinson put it, a thicket of algebra (1962, 112).[6] Neoclassical economics has served as an ideology of governance in post-industrial societies, particularly in English-speaking countries and in relation to the operation of international organisations including the IMF, the World Bank and the World Trade Organization.[7] Crouch (2011) argues that realpolitik neoliberalism has not promoted unfettered markets but rather has led to penetration of government by giant transnational corporations and the shaping of all governance to suit the interests of business as understood by such corporations. There is good evidence for this in relation to privatisation and/or marketisation of public services and the form of international trade agreements which not only treat corporations as real social actors with rights but have sought to remove the resolution of disputes between governments and corporations from national courts to transnational dispute resolution through mechanisms dominated precisely by the interests of corporations themselves.

Neoliberalism replaced Keynesianism as that form of regulation proved unable to cope in western democracies with what Glyn and Sutcliffe (1972) called the 'profits squeeze', that is the effect of the combination of full employment, the welfare state and relatively strong trade unions in reducing the ability of capitalists to manage successful accumulation. The doctrine was abandoned as a principle of governance, most notoriously by the Labour Prime Minister James Callaghan in the late 1970s. Keynesianism managed a compromise between labour and capital. Neoliberalism is all for capital and ownership at the expense of workers in all sectors.

If we look at the economy of the UK in 2016 it has only a small monopoly sector of employment much of which actually intersects with the state sector since it is in armaments and related activities for which the main customer is the UK state itself. Privatised utilities have an ambivalent status here since they operate on the basis of charges, but within a system of regulation and price specification/guarantee enforced and delivered by the state. Privatisation of services with the state still meeting the majority of the bill means that by O'Connor's typology the state sector has not contracted, but in many of these privatised areas, and particularly in social care, union organisation has been eliminated and terms and conditions of work are such that employees belong to the precariat. Indeed, this kind of erosion of rights is being extended widely with part-time zero-hours contracts common for adjunct university teachers and massive assaults on the relative wages/salaries and pensions of public sector and related employees. UK Trade Union membership peaked at about 13 million in 1978 but by 2009 had declined to 7 million. The biggest decline has been in the private sector and by 2011 the proportion of manufacturing employees in a union had fallen to 20 per cent.

It can be argued that O'Connor's 'competitive sector' no longer exists in the form he described. Certainly, there is a great deal of economic activity which competes on priced levels but much, and probably most, no longer takes the form of small local businesses. Instead we have giant corporations, particularly in retail – Amazon, Sports Direct and so on – which pay low wages often subsidised from taxes but are in a price competitive environment. Typically, there are no unions in this sector. There is an overlap with the state sector in that in the UK residential social care has been very largely privatised and there has been a very considerable consolidation of ownership in this sector. Not only is much of the revenue of this sector drawn from taxation through payments by local authorities, the Southern Cross example, where a very large chain care provider failed financially, shows that there has been no transfer of risk. When Southern Cross failed local authorities and the health service were obliged to take on its responsibilities in order to continue to provide residential care. We might argue that the labour relations of O'Connor's competitive sector have become generalised up and into the state sector, but the forms of ownership are very different with Crouch's giant corporations well-embedded in this low wage and high insecurity domain.

Conclusion: benefits and taxes after industry – a post-industrial welfare state?

Perhaps the most indicative change in state activities and expenditure for the industrial/post-industrial transformation is the change in the focus of cash benefits for those of working age. In 2015–16 the anticipated expenditure on benefits for those out of work, that is on Job Seekers' Allowance (JSA) and Employment Support Allowance (ESA), was £17 billion, the bulk of this being ESA which is paid to workers who have incapacities making it more difficult for them to enter the labour market.[8] Tax Credits paid to households including an employed worker were expected to total £30 billion. It is difficult to discover just what part of the £24 billion Housing Benefit bill goes to households with an employed worker but certainly a substantial part – at least a fifth – does. What this indicates is that beginning in the early 1970s with Family Income Support, the UK welfare state has reversed the policy established by the New Poor Law of 1834 which outlawed the payment of wage supplements funded from taxation to low paid workers. This was a gradual move but the introduction of Tax Credits transformed the picture. We have a flexible labour market in which low wages are subsidised by those who pay taxes. Moreover, the conditionalities attached to JSA and even for most recipients to ESA are so strict as to reproduce the logic of the nineteenth century Poor Law rather than the mix of rights and responsibilities inherent in an insurance based system. Conditionality which takes the form of requirements to job seek and sanctioning through benefit withdrawal if this is not done to a satisfactory level now does not just apply to the wholly unemployed. Recipients of the new Universal Credit which is supposed to unify tax and benefits who are working part time can be sanctioned if they are considered to be not actively seeking to increase their hours towards a full-time level. These benefit regimes govern the lives of the precariously employed to a degree far beyond that which prevailed in the era of Keynesian regulation.

The rhetoric of fraudulent claims for benefits has been an important component of UK political discourse in recent years. A House of Commons report (2014) quoted figures from a 2013 survey which showed that the general public believed 24 per cent of all benefits were claimed fraudulently when the real figure is 0.7 per cent. This amounts to a total of £1.7 billion a year. In contrast the 'tax gap' – that is the difference between what is due in tax and is actually collected was estimated by HMRC at £34 billion or 6.4 per cent of tax due. Many authorities consider HMRC's estimate to be far too low. Murphy (2014) estimates that the actual sum of tax avoided or evaded is some £120 billion. Even HMRC estimates that criminal tax evasion and dubious tax avoidance totalled £7.1 billion, more than four times the total of fraudulently claimed benefits. The great differences in estimates here are down to the very different approaches of HMRC and that agency's critics. HMRC has been very soft on avoidance by large corporations and successive governments have failed to introduce a general anti-avoidance principle into tax law.

If we look at UK taxes as an example of the tax structure of a post-industrial state, Pope and Waters (2016, 5) show that of a total of UK tax receipts forecast for 2016–17 of £665.1 billion (37.7 per cent of GDP), the following elements raised these sums and percentages:

- income tax net of tax credits – £182.1 billion – 27.4 per cent
- national insurance – £126.5 billion – 19.0 per cent
- VAT – £120.1 billion – 18.0 per cent
- other indirect taxes – £69.8 billion – 10.8 per cent
- taxes on capital (Stamp Duty providing half of this) – £27.7 billion – 4.2 per cent
- taxes on companies – £73.7 billion – 11.2 per cent
- council tax paid by households – £30.1 billion – 4.5 per cent
- miscellaneous other taxes – £35.4 billion – 5.4 per cent.

Total spending by the UK Department of Work and Pensions (DWP) on benefits which have some sort of 'insurance history'[9] is £152 billion, so national insurance does not pay for this but it does meet the cost of old age pensions at £108 billion.

One very clear illustration of the impact of deindustrialisation on the UK, the world's first and formerly most industrialised nation, is provided by the spatial origins of UK tax revenues. McGough and Piazza (2016) examined the UK's major cities which in 2014–15 generated 64 per cent of all UK taxes. London alone, itself massively deindustrialised but also the centre of UK financial services, generated 68 per cent of this, that is, 44 per cent of taxes collected. This reflects in part the booking of corporation and other taxes at London head offices but it is still a massive proportion. The UK's space economy has become seriously imbalanced away from those regions which generated much of the nation's income and wealth in the industrial era. McGough and Piazza note that in the period between their study and the financial crash tax generated has fallen, particularly in the formerly industrial city regions. They assign this to changes in the character of the labour force:

> The majority of cities (43) generate less income tax today than a decade ago, and of these, the majority (33) have more jobs commanding lower individual wages, suggesting that wage levels have had a more significant impact on tax revenues than employment levels. (2016, 3)

In subsequent chapters we will explore both the implications of this post-industrial tax structure for inequality among households and the implications of the gap between taxes raised and government expenditure – the deficit as this term is generally deployed. Here we will simply note that taxes which have a regressive impact – national insurance, VAT, other indirect taxes and council tax – provide nearly half of the total government revenue.

Notes

[1] Although O'Connor noted the distinctive character of US politics in relation to the absence of a Social Democratic or Labour Party as a significant political actor, he asserted – in our view correctly – that the US still stood as a relevant example for capitalist social orders as a whole.

[2] The content of this section is a summary of the account O'Connor presented in Chapter Two of *The Fiscal Crisis of the State* entitled 'An Anatomy of American State Capitalism'.

[3] See https://stats.oecd.org/Index.aspx?DataSetCode=REVGBR

[4] In general, UK income substitution benefits are now flat rate rather than income related and for those of working age have a shorter period of eligibility before there is an imposition of means testing which takes account of savings and partner's income, and are subject to much more intensive conditionality regimes.

[5] Although private sector unions in the past have resisted tax increases even on capital and even in the UK.

[6] Since the models based on this algebra are essentially linear, they have proved to be completely useless in dealing even in descriptive terms with transformational crisis. Physicists who can at least handle non-linear modelling have developed a school of 'econo-physics' in an effort to transcend this. However, only if this approach can handle messy reality and deal, for example, with the issues raised by institutional economics will it actually prove to be of any real use.

[7] The dominance of the pretty poor education provided by an Oxford degree in Politics (too much psephology), Philosophy (the sterility of the analytical turn), and Economics (the pure nonsense of the neoclassical school) among UK politicians and senior figures across governance has much to answer for in terms of bad policy and bad politics.

[8] ESA's predecessor, Incapacity Benefit, was used by government as a mechanism to smooth the industrial/post-industrial transformation. It was not means tested or time limited, recipients could get some part-time earnings as therapeutic work, and there was no household means test. Essentially it smoothed the transition of many former industrial workers from employment to retirement.

[9] Although in the past a substantial part of this spending would have been outside the insurance principle in the form of National Assistance/ Supplementary benefit. That system was created precisely to cover those who did not have adequate insurance rights *and* to top up inadequate insurance benefits, although Beveridge had hoped to design a system in which benefits were adequate.

TWO

The history of tax and the development of the fiscal crisis in post-industrial capitalism

This chapter will focus on the forms and history of taxation in post-industrial societies. It will begin with a historical review of the forms of taxation in modern states – taxation of real property, of consumption, of capital through taxes on profits, capital gains and wealth inheritance, of incomes and of workers through social insurance. These will be considered in a comparative mode looking at the UK, Germany, France, the USA and Scandinavia. Then we examine the implications for state revenues and budgets of the ability of corporations, very high income individuals and holders of substantial wealth to avoid taxation, either through careful use of the tax codes of their own nations or through international transfer to low tax regimes. The chapter will conclude with a discussion of the issues posed by avoidance for the overall funding of welfare states in relation to the developing fiscal crisis.

The treatment here will differ from conventional discussions of tax in economic treatments as represented by the Mirrlees Report (Mirrlees et al, 2011). We agree with the Schumpeterian imperative that we can best understand states through attention to their budgets but we want to historicise and functionalise it. By 'functionalise', we mean that we want to see what purposes taxes were meant to serve. By 'historicise', we mean that we want to set that functional consideration in relation to historical origins of a tax and consider how things have developed through time. We distinguish here between the use of 'purpose' in this chapter and O'Connor's typology. Here by 'purpose' we mean the set of political and economic objectives which informed the development of a tax, and we recognise as always that these might be multiples of the elements in O'Connor's typology.

It is useful to clarify some important general aspects of tax systems. First, we have to identify the actual entities which are taxed. Individuals are taxed as income earners and/or as contributors to social insurance systems. Capital gains taxes and inheritance taxes also fall on individuals. For income tax there is an important difference between systems which tax income recipients as individuals as in the contemporary UK and those which tax couples in a legal relationship as was the case in the UK before 1990 and is still the case in the USA. Separate taxation of individual incomes is very advantageous for high income couples and is a factor driving increased household inequality in the UK. For indirect and domestic property taxes the taxation unit is the household since it is the household which is the unit of consumption of goods and the occupier of a residence. Corporate entities are liable for corporation taxes, taxes on commercial properties and a range of environmental taxes. Second, we should note the significance of the mode of tax collection. In most systems most employed workers and many occupational pensioners have income and social security taxes withheld from earnings/pensions and paid to the tax collection by their employer or pension fund. These taxes are not invisible since pay notes typically record tax and social insurance paid but for most people what matters is their net income. Out of this are paid indirect taxes which are mostly invisible in that they are collected by the sellers of goods and services and paid to the tax collector by them. Sometimes we can see VAT and of course cash payment to small builders and so on is a mode of tax evasion by both parties. The customer evades VAT and the self-employed worker evades income tax. However, in general those paying indirect taxes are not aware of it. Third, we have the size of the tax base. How many entities are there which are required to pay any particular tax? How many adults are liable for income tax because they have enough income to come over the threshold for its application? How many workers – employed and self-employed – are covered by a social insurance scheme? How many corporate entities are liable for the corporation taxes of any particular national tax system? Are suppliers of goods and services located in a national tax system and therefore liable to pay VAT and/or Corporation Tax? All of these elements differ across systems and within systems across time.

We also need to think about the units which receive cash benefits through social insurance and social assistance systems, since for many households income is a combination of benefits received and taxable income earned or otherwise obtained. There is a move in some systems, particularly the UK, towards an integration of tax and benefit systems. Many social insurance systems take payments from individual workers but actually give benefits on a scale which takes account of recipients' circumstances in relation to the number of dependants. Social assistance benefits in whatever form take account of dependants, so typically the unit for benefits is a single-family household whereas the unit for taxation can be the individual member of that single-family household.

Finally, we need to think in dynamic terms about the actual trajectories through time of the entities which are being taxed as well as the dynamism of tax systems and of the socio-economic systems in which both tax and benefit systems are crucial sub-systems. Individuals have a life course which in contemporary post-industrial societies includes extended periods when incomes from work are either non-existent or low, that is, childhood, adolescence and for the now almost majority who continue to third-level education, young adulthood at one end of the age scale and old age as a retired worker at the other.[1] We need to think about how taxes and benefits work out over this life course recognising that wider system changes mean that future life courses will not be the same as those in the past.[2] Individuals pass their life courses within households but households have a different trajectory from the individuals themselves. This is not just a matter of passage from dependency at a younger age to adulthood and own household establishment. Households dissolve and reform, something recognised in all household panel longitudinal studies where the only constant unit is not the particular household, but rather the individual who often will move through more than one household in the course of an adult life.

As we noted in the introduction to this book, while we have radical disagreements with the neoclassical welfare economics framework which underpins the arguments of the Mirrlees Report (Mirrlees et al, 2011), there is one fundamental assertion made there with which we wholly agree. That is that we have to understand a nation's taxation assemblage as a *system*. The different taxes have to be considered together in relation to their impact and consequences. And, they have to be understood as a system intersecting with other systems, affected by those systems, and affecting them – with causal powers running in all directions. Social security and social assistance are so integrated with tax systems that it is perhaps inappropriate to talk about a tax system but we should rather refer to a tax and benefit system since it is the combination of both which determines the post-tax disposable income of a household.[3] Attempts to integrate tax and benefit systems, like the UK's introduction of Universal Credit, recognise this. And, of course, tax exemptions, what Titmuss (1958) called 'fiscal welfare', contribute to the real incomes of households. If you are allowed not to pay a tax for some reason, you have more to spend elsewhere. This does not apply just to households. It also relates to corporations given the scale of what Farnsworth (2015) has called corporate welfare. We are reiterating our understanding of taxation as a complex system in relation with other complex systems. The point of this reiteration here is that the components of the tax system developed historically to some degree in isolation from each other for specific purposes in specific historical contexts. The system as it stands in any nation state – and with some impacts from transnational governance – is an emergent one. To understand that emergent we have to understand its history and that we will attempt to do in this chapter.

What is taxed: the elements of the tax base

The term 'tax base' refers to what is available to be taxed. We can think of it both in terms of kind, that is what is taxed, and volume – the actual size of each element taken separately and then together. So the elements of any tax base include any or all of taxes on trade – tariffs, taxes on land, taxes on income, taxes on consumption, taxes on environmental impact and taxes on capital/wealth which for us includes taxes on profits in the form of corporation taxes of whatever kind. England and Wales have a history of the development of taxes which can stand as an example against which other nation states can be compared. If we go back to the sixteenth century we find taxation being a matter of customs and related duties which were used to support the activities of the central state as the Crown, particularly in funding the navy and military. There was the special tax of 'ship money' which was to be one of the central points of contention between Parliament and the Crown in the seventeenth century and a factor leading to the Civil War in England.[4] However, there was another very important domain of taxation, the poor rates collected on a parish basis through a tax on real property which funded support for the indigent. Legislation, culminating in the 43rd of Elizabeth of 1602 laid out the arrangements for assessing and levying this tax, which was the basic precursor of tax raised for income maintenance purposes. English parishes were treated as administrative units but the entirely separate Scots Poor Law established in 1574, although modelled in important respects on English legislation, used the religious parish as the unit of collection and allocated half of all church collections to poor relief with any deficit to be collected from landowners as heritors in rural areas and small boroughs and by the magistrates and town councils in large boroughs. An important distinction between the English[5] and Scottish poor law systems was that in England the able bodied could be relieved, whereas in Scotland only the impotent poor were eligible for relief, a distinction that persisted almost to the beginning of the twentieth century and reflected the Calvinist conceptions of worth which dominated Scottish civil society and politics. Both systems were devised to address issues which arose from the Reformation in the respective countries which had eliminated religious sources of relief from monasteries and convents, and at the same time was associated with the enclosure and the elimination of common rights, particularly in England. Enclosure was very important as a legal precursor to the agricultural revolution of the eighteenth century which enabled the development of large towns and the industrial revolution itself. Systems for poor relief in the former English colonies of the United States were based on the English Poor Law although very much coloured by Calvinist attitudes as in Scotland.

A crucial development in the English Poor Law in the late eighteenth century was the introduction of local systems for supplementing the wages of farm labourers on scales based on the size of their families and the price of bread. These are usually known as Speenhamland systems after that introduced in the County of Berkshire in 1795 following a meeting of that county's magistrates[6] in the Pelican Inn in Speenhamland. Polanyi in *The Great Transformation* (1944) regarded this initiative as indicative both of the development of market oriented social relations and of the dominance of a philosophical commitment to market principles in public policy. The tax served immediate practical interests in the rural capitalism of England at that time. It sustained an adequate workforce available at times of high labour demand, particularly at harvest. It also meant that rural labourers could afford to marry and have children, ensuring the reproduction of rural labour power.

Out relief subsidy of low wages lasted in England until the New Poor Law of 1834. A driving factor for that radical shift was the impact of technical innovation in agriculture and in particular the introduction of steam-powered threshing machinery which reduced the need for agricultural labour. The Swing riots (Hobsbawm and Rudé, 1969) were important episodes of social discontent and resistance. Speenhamland had served the purposes both of social expenses and social consumption. It reduced the cost of labour power to capitalist farming, although the tax was levied on land values and hence on that very system, and it served a legitimation purpose. Contemporary commentators often cited Poor Law relief as an explanation for the absence of serious revolutionary potential in England. When both agricultural capitalism and industrial capitalism required a different system, then the system was changed. Under the New Poor Law out relief – that is, relief not given in a workhouse – was banned and there was no subsidy to low wages.[7] The system was informed by the doctrine of laissez faire and the principle of less eligibility, that is relief for the able bodied would be given on terms worse than that of 'the meanest employed labourer'. At this point Ireland had no system of poor relief on a national basis with most of the rural poor dependent on familial and community charity. Ireland, which contained some 30 per cent of the UK's population in 1841, was a poor peasant society with a massive surplus population. This was recognised by the Irish Commission on the Poor Law whose report of 1837 was almost proto-Keynesian in character. However, their recommendations were ignored and the English system was imposed on Ireland, a key factor in the Irish Famine of the 1840s.

In the United States, there was fairly minimal poor relief in the nineteenth century, although Skocpol (1995) notes that the system of federal post-civil war pensions for veterans of the Union Army meant that a large proportion of households in the northern states had a pension income. Republican Federal US administrations used international trade tariffs both to protect developing US industries and as the funding source for these benefits which were very attractive to Republican voters. The role of the Veterans' Administration as a US social policy agency has been considerable and illustrates the significance of what Andreski (1954) called 'the military participation ration' in policy. Old Age pensions delivered on a basis of worth and not on a social insurance basis precede the development of social insurance schemes in the UK (then including all of Ireland) in 1908 and Denmark in 1891. These were means tested but only available to those with a history of respectability and were funded from general taxation rather than a social insurance fund. In contrast German pensions were introduced on an insurance basis as part of Bismark's reforms. The core of US and French pension systems date from the

1930s, again on an insurance basis. The key element of US social insurance remains pensions in old age.

There is a distinction to be made between insurance-based pensions and the original UK and Danish systems. Insurance is insurance against a risk. It is pooled. The risk originally insured for pensions was that of survival to old age when many did not but by the post-Second World War period, most did, even if not always for long. The UK system was associated with Lloyd George's 'people's budget' of 1909, the first fiscal measure in the UK which had the intention of redistributing income. As originally proposed this had included a land value tax[8] as well as increases in tax on higher incomes, but the radical land tax element was lost in a compromise with the House of Lords. Lloyd George intended to erode the power of the landed aristocracy, and death duties, introduced earlier in the 1890s, had the same objective. Theodore Roosevelt was also a strong supporter of inheritance taxes. Redistribution of wealth through taxation was an important political issue in both the UK and USA in the early twentieth century. Death duties are now easily avoided by the very rich. In the UK agricultural land has been exempt from local taxation since the 1920s, is not now usually liable for capital gains taxation and can be exempt from inheritance tax. Lloyd George's budget proposed a tax of 20 per cent on increased value of land on sales, a precursor to post-war Labour's Development Land Charge which originally taxed any gain in land value obtained by a change in use designation under planning proposals at 100 per cent. The Tory government abolished this in the 1950s and although subsequent Labour governments reintroduced a version of it, it was finally abolished by the Thatcher government in the 1980s. This means that public bodies can no longer acquire land at existing use value for public purposes and has massively distorted land markets since value derived from permitted use is now dominant as opposed to any rational base for valuation in relation to current use.

Property taxes in the UK were originally funders of local poor relief but with the development of local service provision in public health and education as well as policing they became more general in their function. The UK now funds most municipal services from national taxation with redistribution among responsible bodies on the basis of formula funding.[9] These formulae are intended to redistribute resources in relation to need but have been regularly adjusted in ways which reflect both political priorities and the desire of central governments to reward areas which support them in elections. School funding in the US is to a considerable extent dependent on local property taxes. Federal government allocates funds to states and states use some of their own tax revenue in addition to this in funding schools but the redistributive mechanisms are weak and poorer school districts have much less funding than affluent areas. In general, across post-industrial countries, unless there is some strong redistributive mechanism then for any service which depends on a local property taxation base, poorer localities have less well-funded systems.

Taxes on income include social insurance systems which redistribute horizontally, that is, among potential recipients. For this reason, they are often considered to be not part of the tax system. A crucial issue is the degree to which receipt of benefits, including, in many countries, healthcare, is dependent on contribution record. In the UK this link is now almost wholly broken and national insurance is simply a tax on earnings. Elsewhere, for example Germany, the link is much stronger. Nonetheless it is sensible to regard social insurance payments as part of public expenditure since they are backed up by state guarantees.

In the depression of the 1930s locally funded systems for the relief of poverty broke down as long-term unemployed people exhausted their insurance rights and turned to them. This led to national interventions, in the UK in the form of the Unemployment Assistance Board funded from general taxation, which became National Assistance in the post-Second World War welfare state. Social Insurance payments are a tax on earned incomes. This is as true of employers' contributions as it is of employees since social insurance payments are part of the cost of employing labour, of the wage bill. Payments by the self-employed vary widely, both among countries and over time, but generally they make a payment which offers some but not all of the rights assigned to the employed worker. For them, as for employees, social insurance is a tax on income. It is often not considered properly in discussions of taxation and there have been proposals, for example by Richard Crossman in the 1960s, to increase it because people do not recognise it as a tax – an attempt to con workers which actually has been done given that the link between contribution and benefits in the UK is now very weak and the tax is regressive in relation to not only the earned incomes of the highly paid but also as a tax not levied on 'unearned income'.[10] In the USA three-quarters of taxpayers pay more in payroll taxes funding social insurance which originated with the New Deal Federal Insurance Contribution Act than they do in income tax. As in the UK this has a regressive character as contributions come only from earned incomes below a capped level and are not levied on unearned incomes.

Income tax as such was originally introduced as a tax only on high incomes. Lloyd George's budget of 1909 proposed a progressive income tax which would not affect the great majority of workers but rose for very high incomes. Income tax in the UK only started to be paid by most households during the Second World War. The number of tax paying families[11] rose from 4.8 million in 1938–39 to 14.5 million in 1948–49. By 2015–16 there were more than 30 million income tax payers in the UK which is about 60 per cent of the adult population, although Pope and Waters (2016, 55) have calculated that 73 per cent of adults live in household which pays income tax. This is also roughly the proportion of adult population paying Federal Income Tax in the USA where in many states and municipalities there are additional state or local income taxes as well. The two major drivers for the extension of the coverage of income taxes have been wars and fiscal drag – the failure of governments to raise tax liability thresholds in line sometimes even with inflation and generally in relation to increases in real incomes. In 2016–17 there were projected to be 4.4 million UK tax payers paying the higher rate of income tax at the margin and there were 333,000 tax payers paying the highest (additional) rate. Higher rate tax payers would pay 38.5 per cent of all income tax raised and those paying the highest rate 27.9 per cent.[12] Titmuss in *Income Distribution and Social Change* (1965) showed how various tax allowances advantage higher rate tax payers since any allowance usually has an impact on the marginal tax rate paid. There have been efforts to address this. In the UK before its abolition, for a period, tax relief on mortgage interest paid in connection with the purchase of own main home was set at the standard tax rate, but many allowances, and in particular those for payments to pension schemes, are usually at the marginal rate.

Tax relief for mortgage interest raises the important question of what constitutes income which can be taxed. Owners of a domestic property can do either of two things with it. They can live in it themselves as an owner-occupier or they can rent it to somebody else as a landlord. If they rent it out then the rent is treated as income and is liable for income tax. The general principle that any expense incurred in earning an income is allowable against the tax liability on that income means that the interest charged on a loan raised to purchase or improve the property[13] is allowable as an expense. Until 1963 in the UK the income in kind which an owner-occupier obtained by living in the property was regarded as an income which could be taxed under Schedule A taxation although the valuation which was used to calculate the liability was very much out of date. This was a good method of avoiding distortions in housing markets by not giving owner-occupation a privileged position over renting. So owner-occupiers were allowed to charge interest on loans raised to purchase the property on the same basis as landlords. When the tax was abolished the relief was maintained for more than 30 years because abolition of it was electorally unpopular and governments wanted to encourage owner-occupation. Some other incomes in kind are still taxed, for example, company cars as a benefit. The principle is sound. The practice is varied and inadequate.

Taxes paid by corporate entities, that is for profit enterprises having the legal rights involved in incorporation, are another important source of income for nation states and in some federal systems also for lower levels of governance. Tax on the corporate entity can be treated separately from tax on income distributed to owners in whatever form of the capital in that corporate entity. At some points both have been taxed although post-war UK Labour governments taxed distributed profits at a higher rate than profits retained within a firm in an effort to encourage firms to retain profits as a basis for future investment. Generally, in the UK before the Blair governments Labour was in favour of taxing both corporate income and distributed income, for example, dividends, while Conservative governments treated this as double taxation and introduced mechanisms to avoid it. The US Federal corporate taxation has generally taken the classical form and taxed both profits at the corporate level and distributed dividend income as income of recipients, although there have been variations in this over time. In Germany in addition to corporation tax at the federal level, municipalities are entitled to charge a trade tax on liable profits within a range of rates set by the federal government. This is best regarded as a local version of corporation tax. Some US states have state corporation taxes of the same kind.

There are two issues in relation to tax avoidance around taxation of corporate entities. The first is the ability of corporations to reduce their rate of liable corporation tax by locating their corporate headquarters in low taxation states or by using intra organisational pricing and loan mechanisms to relocate profits to elements within their own structure located in such states. At the other end of the scale self-employed workers can set up firms to which their earnings are paid. They can then appoint household members as directors and/or shareholders and split income tax liability in this way as well as use other methods for reducing tax liability. This approach is commonly used by high income media personnel including those who are presenters and reporters on publicly funded broadcast media.

One element of taxation which is specifically targeted at redistribution is the set of taxes in France and Germany referred to as Solidarity Taxes. In France, this includes a tax on wealth of more than €1.3 million. Some elements of wealth, notably the capital value of pension pots, are excluded. In 2007 this brought in €4.42 billion, 1.5 per cent of France's total tax receipts. France's General Social Contribution, a tax of 7.5 per cent on earned income and 8.2 per cent on unearned income (2007) funds health, family benefits and the social solidarity retirement fund. This also has solidarity functions and raised €75 billion. It was the second most important tax in France after VAT. In Germany, a progressive solidarity surcharge is levied on higher incomes on all of income tax, withholding taxes (social security contributions), and capital yields tax.

Table 2.1: International comparisons

Indicator	Denmark	France	Germany	USA	UK
% GDP all taxes 2014	46.7	43.0	35.6	26.9	31.7
2014 Taxes on Income and Profits % GDP	33.2	10.5	11.6	11.4	12.5
% Taxes Central Government 2013	73.3	33.6	31.4	41.2	75.8
% Taxes state / region 2013	-	-	21.9	20.2	75.8
% Total Taxes municipal 2013	26.3	12.9	8.2	14.5	4.9
% Total Tax Personal Income 2013	54.8	18.6	26.1	38.7	27.7
% Total Tax Corporation 2013	5.6	5.7	4.9	8.5	7.7
% Total Tax Social Security 2013	0.2	37.2	38.1	18.8	24.2
Total Tax Property 2013	3.9	8.4	2.5	11.3	12.3
% Total Tax on Goods and Services 2013	32.3	24.1	28.0	17.4	32.9
Gini Disposable Income 2013	0.254	0.294	0.292	0.396	0.358
Gini Market Income 2013	0.442	0.504	0.508	0.513	0.527

Source: www.oecd.org › Tax › Tax policy analysis

Table 2.1 shows the general pattern of taxation across a range of post-industrial nation states. Of particular interest is the relationship between the proportion of GDP taken in taxes on the one hand and the difference between market income and disposable income Gini coefficients on the other. The Gini coefficient is a measure of inequality in an income distribution across a population which varies between a value of 1 – one income unit has all the income – and zero – all income units have exactly the same income. Market income is all income excluding cash benefits and before the impact of taxes. Disposable income is income after taxes and including cash benefits. Plainly the higher the tax take as a proportion of GDP the more equal disposable incomes become. The UK which is more unequal in terms of market income than the USA but is more equal in terms of disposable income. Other European countries become more equal than either. Denmark, the most equal in terms of disposable income of all OECD states, has a more equal market income and a very high tax take. Market income does not take account of tax avoidance since it is based on incomes declared for tax purposes.

Taxes not paid: the role of allowances and avoidance/evasion

Tax systems generally include a set of allowances that is, elements which would normally be taxed but are not. We should distinguish allowances from expenses. Expenses are costs incurred in obtaining the income. Allowances are consequences of policies which exempt an element which would otherwise be taxed. These are not confined to income taxes. Across Europe there are elements of consumption which are not taxed for VAT. Typically food purchases do not incur a VAT charge. In the UK, single person households receive a 25 per cent discount on the Council Tax, the property tax on their dwelling. Receipt of income tax allowances is generally automatic that is, eligibility is determined by the information provided to the tax authorities. The issue is not allowances per se but rather that in any progressive tax system allowances are usually worth much more to higher rate tax payers since they push up the income level at which the higher rate tax becomes payable. Allowances constitute what Titmuss (1958) called 'the fiscal welfare state'. Sinfield (2016) calculated that tax expenditures that is, tax foregone through allowances in the UK for 2015–16 would turn out at some £92 billion and this does not include an estimate of the value of personalising the income tax liability of each member of a couple. Allowances are entirely legal, the product of policies – albeit a set of poorly connected and ad hoc policies – and not of the same deliberate and calculated form as either the pursuit of legal tax avoidance or the criminal attempt to evade taxes. Nonetheless they are there and have a regressive effect.

We have to distinguish between tax evasion which is a criminal offence in which taxes are avoided by non-declaration or moving income and/or assets outside the scope of tax collection in a way which is clearly illegal, and tax avoidance which is the use made of what appear to be legal modes of reducing the tax liability of individuals, corporations or estates. Far more staff are employed in the UK by DWP to investigate benefit fraud than are employed by HRMC in pursuit of major tax evasion and often large-scale tax evaders get away very lightly. For example, of more than 1,000 holders of illegal Swiss bank accounts, only one was prosecuted and most got away with what were widely regarded as very low penalties. The whole issue of tax avoidance and evasion has been brought into public debate primarily by the Tax Justice Network[14] and much of what follows is based on either the publications of this estimable organisation or on press stories stimulated by its work, particularly Murphy and Christensen's *Tax Us if you Can* (2013) and Massey et al's *The Greatest Invention: Tax and the Campaign for a Just Society* (2015). We refer interested readers to those texts for the full horrific story of how the rich avoid taxes. Some aspects and illustrations of tax evasion/avoidance have been presented in this chapter so far. Here we want to simply comment on the big picture. There are two aspects to this in post-industrial industrial capitalism. One is the development over time of an entire industry of tax avoidance (see Sikka, 2015), much of it having its origins and indeed its contemporary location in that anomaly of governance, the City of London, and using both the UK itself and a range of other tax havens. The other is the shift in governments' attitudes to tax collection. In English speaking countries not only has there been a widespread reduction in tax rates both on high income individuals and on corporations, but there has been a marked weakening of enforcement mechanisms. In the UK this began in the 1980s with the Thatcher governments at a time when, as Alt et al (2010) observed, 'the large cuts in statutory rates of [UK] income tax took place at a time when attitudes to redistribution were at their most favourable, and when a majority of voters voted for parties who did not favour these cuts' (p 1205).

It was not just that tax rates were cut. The mechanisms for collection were softened up in relation not only to large corporations but also the wealthy. In the US, for example, in the early 2000s most audits by the IRS were of individual tax payers but the 3 per cent that were of corporations raised 80 per cent of the taxes collected as a consequence of audits. Sweetheart deals with very large corporations have become a public issue in the UK where the House of Commons Public Accounts' Committee has questioned them in the most severe terms, without however achieving – at least so far – much in the way of change in practice.

Murphy and Christensen explain why tax collection is so important in contemporary post-industrial societies:

> [prior to the financial crash of 2008] there appeared to be enough tax revenue to go round. Many of the problems we addressed [in the first edition] could be ignored by politicians, or at least papered over by throwing cash at the problem. This is no longer the case: tax revenues are among the scarcest commodities in most countries. It is that shortage of tax revenue and not excessive state spending, which has plunged public finances around the world into deficit. (2013, 2)

We will brutally summarise the arguments of this most important text. Murphy and Christensen reckon that globally some $US 21 trillion to $US 32 trillion[15] is avoided/evaded. The tax loss was at least $US

3 trillion and 25 per cent of this was taxes otherwise due within the European Union. This happens because tax policies and enforcement regimes remain national while financial systems can take advantage of a globalised market.[16] There are a multiplicity of ways in which all sorts of taxes can be avoided. The establishment of Trust mechanisms neutered the intentions of UK inheritance tax; the ability to hold non-domiciled status for citizens (other than in the US) means that very wealthy and/or high income individuals can avoid income tax; the ability of companies to relocate profits to low tax regimes has meant that companies can pay minimal corporation tax against massive revenues; tax havens grant citizenship to very wealthy individuals who receive income there – for example Monaco to Lady Green, wife of Sir Philip, the former owner of UK's British Home Stores who received £1.2 billion from Arcadia in 2005.[17] In 2012 the UK National Audit Office reported that HMRC were investigating some 41,000 tax avoidance schemes. Murphy and Christensen sum it up like this: 'Taxing locally when companies [and very wealthy individuals and families] act globally has given rise to a crisis in taxing capital. For the sake of economic justice, that crisis must now be addressed' (2013, 37).

It is worthwhile asking how democracies which in the fortunate third quarter of the twentieth century saw considerable redistribution, the development of effective welfare states, and large reductions in inequality have come to this state. Much of this must be considered in terms of the consequences of massive structural change, of the shift from industrial to post-industrial capitalism. However, we cannot ignore the activities of individuals and corporate entities, particularly the very large global accountancy firms, in relation to all of political funding, lobbying, funding of market promoting think tanks, and in particular the new merry-go-round in which public officials not only move on into the private sector but now move from the private sector into government. An extreme example is that of Edward Troup, now Executive Chair of HMRC who was a tax partner in a large firm of solicitors, a special advisor to the Tory Chancellor Ken Clark, and then returned to the private sector before being brought back by New Labour in 2004 to the Treasury in a tax role, taking on the overall directorship in relation to tax and welfare in 2010. In 1997 Troup was reported as describing tax as legalised extortion and spent much of his career in the private sector in a firm which has a record of advising corporations on how to reduce their tax bills by the use of tax havens and other means. Thompson, the current Chief Executive and Permanent Secretary at HMRC, has had a career primarily in the public service in local and central government but was for a period in the private sector including employment with Ernst and Young, one of the global big four audit and accountancy firms which is very much engaged with tax avoidance. Of course, politicians also move into the private sector and both New Labour Chancellors, Brown and Darling, now have roles in global finance, Brown with global asset manager PIMCO[18] and Darling with the bank Morgan Stanley.

Shaxon and Christensen (2013) identify what they call 'The Finance Curse' which they equate with the national resources curse long identified in development studies. Third World countries rich in natural resources often fail to achieve development goals because there is widespread corruption, not least in the form of tax evasion. Likewise, countries with overdeveloped financial sectors, notably the UK with the City of London, suffer. This rings absolutely true. Brown as New Labour Chancellor was very much in awe of the City and seemed to consider it the driver of the UK economy and the potential source of tax revenues for redistribution. We will go into where that got us in the next chapter but it is plain that New Labour had no coherent industrial policy to speak of, massively neglected its own electoral heartlands in former coalfield and heavy industrial areas, and continued the process of deindustrialisation reinforced by active policy and passive neglect which had characterised the Thatcher years. So we have the post-industrial fiscal *and* political *and* cultural crisis. To that we turn in Chapter Three.

Notes

[1] The status of non-employed housewife/non-working mother is now much less common.

[2] This is particularly true in relation to the lifetime income implications of a third-level education.

[3] Disposable indicates what people have to spend. Post-tax takes account of what proportion of that expenditure goes on the payment of indirect taxes.

[4] The Civil War in Scotland was about issues of religious organisation and theological principles. These mattered in England but tax mattered more.

[5] English law applied in Wales.

[6] Magistrates had oversight administrative responsibility for the Poor Law.

[7] Since the 1970s the UK has developed a new Speenhamland system for subsidising low wages from tax revenues. This began with Family Income Supplement and means tested reliefs of rent charges and local taxation charges but has now extended massively with the development of tax credits and the turn towards a Universal Credit system. The irony is that the rural capitalists who developed Speenhamland actually paid the taxes which subsidised low wages. Many of the companies which benefit so massively from subsidisation of contemporary low wages are noted tax avoiders. In 2015 it was reported that Amazon paid just £11.9 million corporation tax on £5.3 billion of UK sales but the same company pays below the living wage in the UK to many of its workers who are eligible for tax-funded supplements to their low wages. These come from the taxes paid by individuals, households and companies which actually pay their taxes due unlike Amazon which utilises Luxemburg as a tax shelter.

[8] Based on Henry George's proposals for a single tax – the main platform of Social Credit Parties in the interwar years.

[9] Although recent grant settlements have pushed the enactment of austerity in considerable part down to the local government level and are forcing local authorities to increase local taxation. This is a major shift in the UK tax base and will have grave consequences for inequalities in service provision.

[10] An expression which should always be deployed in discussions of taxation.

[11] Until 1990 couples were taxed jointly. The introduction of individual taxation in that year has been of enormous advantage to double income families with relatively high incomes.

[12] These were the takes not just from the higher and highest marginal tax rates but from the total tax paid by these categories. Source: www.gov.uk/government/statistics/income-tax-liabilities-statistics-tax-year-2013-to-2014-to-tax-year-2016-to-2017

[13] And costs of maintenance.

[14] See www.taxjustice.net/

[15] A trillion is one thousand billion. These very large numbers are hard to grasp so here is a way to do it. Turn it into time. A million seconds is about 12 days. A billion seconds is 31.7 years. A trillion seconds is 31,709.8 years.

[16] Although at this point (August 2016) the European Union has gone after €14.5 billion which Apple has avoided through a special tax arrangement with the Irish government. Ireland has one of the lowest tax rates – 12.5 per cent – in the EU but Apple has paid far less than this – 0.005 per cent. The EU Commission asserts that this rate is illegal and Apple must pay at least the 12.5 per cent rate.

[17] Green was knighted for services to retail by New Labour.

[18] Brown pays his fees into his charitable foundation but still relies on global finance capital for these fees.

THREE

Austerity, debt and welfare in post-industrial capitalism

The phrase 'the age of austerity' sums up the nature of politics and policy across post-industrial capitalism in the aftermath of the financial crash of 2008. Let us be absolutely clear as to the origins of the contemporary crisis. They do not lie in over expenditure by states in the years before 2008. They derive entirely and absolutely from the behaviour of the banks and if governments share in the responsibility, this is not because they spent too much on the welfare states but because they failed to regulate financial speculation. Blyth in his magisterial *Austerity: The History of a Dangerous Idea* puts it like this: 'The crisis was generated by the private sector but it is being paid for by the public sector, that is by you and me' (2013a, 22).

What this means is well expressed by Farnsworth and Irving:

Governments have emerged from 2009 with gaping holes in national finances, which are to be filled not through the impact of tax increases on corporations, financial interests and the well off, that is the authors of the crisis story, but by increasing taxes on middle and low income groups and by making swingeing cuts in public expenditure, primarily social welfare. (2011, 20)

For Blyth, the driving force has been an ideology of neoliberalism although critics in a symposium addressing his book identify other factors at the level of the macro economy and the character of political and governance actions (*Comparative European Politics,* 11, 3). From a complexity frame of reference we might argue that all of these were in operation but that Blyth perhaps ought (as Streeck, 2013b, despite being identified as a Weberian by Blyth, suggests) to go back to his Marxist roots and pay attention to the determinant role of the mode of production.[1] However, the ideology of neoliberalism does matter and we need to define this term. Crouch has done this for us:

> one dominant theme is that free markets in which individuals maximize their material interests provide the best means for satisfying human aspirations and that markets are in particular to be preferred over states and politics, which are at best inefficient and at worst threats to freedom. (2011, vii)

This egregious nonsense has been spouted throughout the history of capitalism and despite the fundamental destruction, time and again (see for example Robinson 1962) of its puny intellectual foundations in rather trivial, largely linear, deductive mathematical modelling, it continues, not least through the operation of think tanks like the UK Institute of Economic Affairs,[2] to dominate the intellectual climate of policy makers in the English-speaking world.[3]

We are not going to reproduce here an account of the detailed origins of the crisis in the operations of finance capital and the failure of states to regulate those operations. For that see Blyth. We will simply reiterate the core of Blyth's description. The cost of saving the financial systems post-2008 has been somewhere between $US 3 and $US 13 trillion – the very width of this range illustrates the chaotic nature of the process – and:

> Much of this has ended up on the balance sheets of governments as they absorb the costs of the bust, which is why we mistakenly call this a sovereign debt crisis when in fact it is a transmuted

and well-camouflaged banking crisis…Having already bailed out the banks, we have to make sure there is room on the public balance sheet to backstop them. That's why we have austerity. It's all about saving the banks. (Blyth, 2013a, 5 and 7)

If we are considering only the proximate cause of austerity as policy then Blyth is quite right, but we have to go back beyond proximate causes to see what systemic factors lie behind the phase shift which has generated a capitalism, capitalist politics and capitalist states dedicated to austerity and the destruction of the welfare states of the previous system state of what was industrial capitalism in the west.

Streeck, whose careful characterisation of what how he calls the tax states of Fordist welfare capitalism evolved into first debt states and then consolidation states (2013) will inform subsequent discussion in this chapter, fixes the blame firmly on: 'the long-term decline in the growth performance of advanced capitalist economies and their subsequent inability to honour the promises of economic and human progress on which their legitimacy depended' (2013a, 2).

Again, we agree but what lies behind this decline in growth performance? After all, the last quarter of the twentieth century was one of massive technological innovation, historically the driver of very rapid growth in productivity within industrial capitalism. For us there were a range of inter-related causal drivers of this low growth. First, there was the massive shift in production of material goods outwith advanced industrial capitalist states in the west. This was a globalisation of production with much growth potential transferred to low wage economies with weak or practically non-existent trade union movements operating under authoritarian regimes, not least that of the Chinese communist party. Second there was the shift in focus of capital accumulation in the west towards the secondary circuit of capital. Most writing on this which deals with the appropriation of surplus value in the sphere of circulation rather than production has focused on space and real estate (Lefebvre, 1991; Harvey, 1999). Speculation in real estate in all its forms, including both massive booms in the value of residential dwellings and a shift across post-industrial capitalism towards 'property led regeneration' as the solution to the problems caused by deindustrialisation in formerly industrial cities, is important in and of itself. This is especially true in relation to its impact on politics at the level of localities and regions and in the way in which governance functions in the everyday worlds of lived experience. Feagin (1987) noted how accumulation in the real estate sphere was fuelling accumulation through financial transactions, a prescient observation given the role of financial derivatives based on the securitisation of mortgages in triggering the 2008 crash.

This is an example of what Aalbers (2016) calls the quaternary circuit of capital:

> Financialization not only implies the Financialization of existing economies – i.e. the restructuring of existing economies into producer and consumer markets that are heavily tied to financial markets – but also the rise of financial markets for their own good; that is the rise of financial markets not for the facilitation of other markets but for the trade in money, credit, securities etc. Or, in the words of Cox (1992, 29), finance is increasingly becoming 'decoupled from production to become an independent power, an autocrat over the real economy.

Aalbers argues that the rules of capital accumulation have been rewritten with control over capital shifting from corporate boardrooms taking production decisions to financial markets since even non-financial firms have become enmeshed with financial markets. This is why Castells has called this process 'the mother of all accumulations' (1996, 473). It is important to recognise that taxation policy has become subject to the logics of quaternary accumulation and the politics which derives from this. One key factor in this was a belief that financial services were the main cash cow for government expenditures. Blyth (2013a, 42) asserts that 25 per cent of UK taxes came out of the financial sector and that this was a strong motivation in Brown's rescue of the banks. This figure is wrong. At its peak in 2005–06 the banking sector provided nearly 20 per cent of corporation tax receipts and this dropped to 3.9

per cent in 2011–12 although by 2015–16 it had climbed back to 7.4 per cent (HMRC, 2016b). However, corporation tax generated a small proportion of total tax receipts. In 2014–15 the financial sector as a whole in terms of taxes borne and taxes collected[4] generated 11 per cent of UK taxes with 3.4 per cent of the UK workforce and even before the crash the 2007 estimate was 13.9 per cent (City of London Corporation, 2015). Blyth's overestimate indicates the power of the financial sector in forming public conceptions. Certainly, he is right in saying that Brown's model of social redistribution was based on collecting taxes from the financial sector to fund social policy interventions. That said the oil and gas sector even with its downturn delivered 5.5 per cent of taxes collected in 2012 and Financial Services in 2015–16 delivered just 17.7 per cent of corporation tax on its own.

The UK suffers from being both an oil dependent economy over many years without Norway's creation of a sovereign wealth tax coupled with Norway's history of high redistributive taxation *and* the dominance in economic life of financial services often described in corporate terms as the 'City of London', although much of London's financial services are now located outwith the City's historical boundaries. One aspect of the financialisation of the UK economy is the contemporary dominance of London represented by the more than a quarter of UK tax revenue generated in the Greater London Council area compared with London's 15 per cent share of UK population. Both of these factors – oil and finance – have contributed to the particularly intense deindustrialisation of the UK given their long-term impact on the rate of exchange and the way in which revenues from them allowed governments from 1979 onwards to abandon anything which looked like a coherent industrial policy.

Proponents of austerity have succeeded in asserting a narrative of the need for cuts in public expenditure in order to resolve government debt crises across the post-industrial world. In no small part this has been due to the Labour and Social Democratic parties' manifest failure to oppose the narrative. UK Labour in particular seemed incapable of imagining anything other than 'austerity light'. Writers in a broadly Keynesian tradition argue that from the point of view of macroeconomic management the austerity narrative peddles a fallacy of composition. That is to say it argues that what would resolve a debt problem for an individual – spend less – works at the level of the whole economy. Rather reduced consumption causes the vicious cycle of the multiplier in which less consumption leads to less production which leads to less income and so on.[5] The alternative would be stimuli to production through increased government expenditure particularly on infrastructural projects but also generally with a view to seeing both growth and acceptable levels of inflation cutting debt if debt was thought to be unmanageable.

Streeck (2013a) demonstrates how the expansion of welfare in advanced capitalist democracies in the fortunate third quarter of the twentieth century was associated with continued real growth in those economies over that whole period. The period was characterised by a politics of 'the mixed economy' and full employment. In Germany, the dominant intellectual position was Ordoliberalism[6] which accepted the necessity for the regulation of markets to some degree, exactly in order to sustain the continued existence of market economies. The crucial term associated with that school was the idea of a social market economy – markets free other than in relation to specific and limited regulation with a high level of welfare sustained by an extensive social insurance system. At the time command economies seemed to represent a real alternative to market economies. The German Social Democrats were originally committed to a socialised economic system, although in practice first and then in principle they adopted the social market economy model.

In the UK and France nationalised industries formed an important part of the productive economy, unemployment levels were only frictional, and welfare provision grew under parties of the Centre Left and Centre Right. There was a radical change at the end of the 1970s, which Streeck dates as the beginning of a neoliberal political hegemony. The subsequent general marketisation and financialisation of the old industrial economies and the neoliberal demand for market hegemony across the whole social sphere dominated political and media debate.[7] The radical change in public finances which originated in this period was the growth in public debt as a proportion of GDP, although as Streeck demonstrates, this was part of a massive growth in aggregate debt (including personal debts and corporate debt). Across OECD countries Streeck (2013a, 3) shows that public debt grew from about 40 per cent of GDP in the 1980s to more than 90 per cent at the time of the crash. Growth in debt did level off in the 1990s but has increased again rapidly since the financial crisis. He dismisses scornfully the arguments of public choice theory to the effect that this growth reflects the pressures of mass political demands mediated through democratic processes:

> Summing up, the rise of public debt – the arrival of the debt state – was part of a neoliberal revolution in the post-war political economy. At a time when democratic–redistributive intervention in capitalist markets became ineffectual on many fronts, it is unlikely that increasing public debt can be explained by voters and workers exercising superior political power. Indeed, rather than electorates extracting unearned incomes from the economy, growing government indebtedness in OECD nations was accompanied by a lasting decline in both living conditions and the distributional position of popular majorities, which in turn was associated with a secular decay in the power resources...of redistributive democracy. (Streeck, 2013a, 6)

The decline in the wage share (share of national income paid out in wages) in many deindustrialised countries, examined in more detail later, adds further substance to Streeck's argument. The process has moved through the development of the debt state into what Streeck describes as 'the consolidation state' where the maintenance of investor confidence becomes paramount (2013a, 16). Streeck's interpretation of the 'politics of austerity' is wholly convincing. He identifies it as absolutely a politics of public debt, with not only national governments engaged – as with the Coalition and now Tory UK government's commitment to deficit reduction – but also with supra-national actors and, in particular, the European Union through its monetary union, as with the current case of Greece.

> The politics of public debt may be conceived in terms of a *distributional conflict between creditors and citizens*...Both have claims on public funds in the form of contractual-commercial and political-social rights, respectively. In a democracy, citizens have the possibility of electing a government responsive to them but 'irresponsible' from the viewpoint of financial markets, in the extreme case a government that expropriates its creditors by annulling its debt. As accumulated debt increases, and investors are required to be more careful about where they put their money, creditors will seek guarantees that expropriation will not happen to them; in effect, that their claims will always be given priority over those of citizens, for example of pensioners demanding the pension that the state and employers promised them when they were workers. (2013a, 14)

Streeck identifies a range of proximate causes for these changes in terms of the impact of recession in the 1970s: increasing and increasingly effective tax resistance by corporations and the very rich, especially in the USA where unreformed campaign financing gives both enormous political power; the welfare costs of unemployment or rather non-employment; and declining political participation especially by the lower income sections of society. Behind all this he identifies the ultimate cause of growth in debt as being the declining growth performance of these economies in the second quarter of the twentieth century. By contrast, a complexity take on this transformation is to regard all these as interactive causes which in combination contribute to a socio-economic phase shift in system state. The combination of the ending of the post-war reconstitution of the capital stock of those countries which had seen it so damaged by that war, globalisation and the ideological assault of the neoliberals, all are part of the scenario. Massive tax avoidance facilitated by rogue states is a key factor in the complex and interactive causal mix.

Very high levels of government debt in proportion to national GDPs were not considered problematic prior to the 2008 crash and in practical terms they are not seen as problematic by markets now. Government debts were embedded within a very general rise in overall debt as companies and individuals/households increased their indebtedness in a process described by Crouch (2000) as privatised Keynesianism. Far from markets avoiding government securities they continue to be purchased at terms which are based not so much on the actual economic performance of nation states or on the actual success of governments in reducing debt ratios. Rather what matters is the capacity of governments to service and repay debt. Hence the emergence of the consolidation state.

Streeck and others recognise that one aspect of the neoliberal dominance of contemporary politics goes beyond the general principle of shrinking the share of resources utilised by the state. The adoration of markets extends to the form of provision of services funded from taxation. There has been a massive drive towards privatisation of delivery, with the ideal being presented as states at whatever level simply determining the prospectuses for bids to deliver services and choosing private (or third sector but in practice seldom) contractors on the basis of bids submitted. Even in the UK where there was more direct delivery of services by the national or local state than in most industrial welfare states, there was always a large element of private sector involvement. Historically this was mostly in relation to construction or similar infrastructure delivery and even there many local authorities maintained 'direct labour organisations', that is, their own building operations. An important and well recognised rationale for this was to ensure that cartels of private providers had a public-sector competitor in bidding processes so that price fixing rings would not be able to operate. However, health and social care in particular were almost entirely provided directly by what in Marxist terms we might call devalorised labour. That means that no profit was extracted from the labour of the workers engaged in the task.

The mantra of markets was justified by the assertion that markets ensured efficiency with no regard paid to any of the issues raised by transaction costs; returns to scale – big organisations can deliver many services at a lower unit cost with the bigger the cheaper which leads to natural monopolies – exactly the rationale behind the creation of a unitary social insurance system in place of multiple providers in the UK in 1946, and the reality in the actual economic world as opposed to abstract modelling of imperfect competition. Not only was the mantra of markets asserted in important areas such as the UK's adoption of the private finance initiative (PFI) for the delivery and management of large capital projects such as hospital and school building, but also the accountancy treatment systematically underestimated the cost of the private provider against an alternative public delivery process. In particular, no account whatsoever was taken of the potential, almost invariably realised, for PFI consortia to engage in 'financial engineering' and to transfer their profits to tax havens thus depriving the UK exchequer of revenues (for example, Whitfield, 2016). Although not a PFI deal as such, the sale of the then Inland Revenues' buildings to a financial entity located in Bermuda in order to avoid UK tax was perhaps the most farcical illustration of this process.

There is a good way to understand the drive towards privatisation of the public sector and it has nothing to do with the supposed efficiency of markets. We should turn to Hobhouse's theory of Imperialism as enthusiastically endorsed by no less than Lenin. This was developed in the early twentieth century at the height of actual imperialist competition. Imperialism is not only a matter of expanding potential markets for goods produced on capitalist terms, although that matters, of course. It also involves the bringing of labour previously working in a non-valorised fashion, that is not generating profit as surplus value, into capitalist forms of production. So the extensive privatisation of the English National Health Service expands the areas in which capital can sell its product to consumers, or even the monopsonist – single buyer – consumer of the state using tax revenues to fund the purchases. It also brings many workers into the process of generating surplus value and profits to generate healthcare as a commodity which is sold rather than a service which is provided, even if the user of the service gets it free at the point of need. Taxes pay the costs and the costs include the profits. In a complex system of health and social care there is no evidence whatsoever that markets make meaningful efficiency savings. Savings are generated by reducing standards of care and driving down the wages and conditions of workers, an important factor in reducing standards themselves. In fact, markets increase operational costs and when there is privatisation the profits element drives costs up even further.

The mention of health and care draws attention to another driver of the fiscal crisis of the post-industrial welfare state. Developments in public health across the 150 years since the introduction of meaningful public health interventions in the 1840s and the antibiotic revolution's impact on mortality from infectious diseases across the life course have led to massive increases in survival rates into old age. Pension systems were predicated on actuarial calculations which did not allow for the period of post-retirement life which is now normal in post-industrial welfare capitalist states. One response to this has been the adjustment of retirement ages both in social insurance funded pensions and in other schemes, not least important of which are the occupational pensions of state employees. If future potential pension liabilities are factored in to calculations of public debt, then that debt rises enormously. In 2015 UK national debt was 81.6 per cent of GDP but if public sector pension liabilities are included then that adds £1.2 trillion to the debt, pushing the ratio up to more than 150 per cent of GDP. Pension schemes can be altered by pushing up retirement ages and reducing the real value of benefits. The other consequences of longer life spans are harder to manage. Improvements in medical technologies have brought a large number of expensive forms of treatment into the repertoire of medical interventions. These can cost a great deal at any stage of the life course – for example life extending expensive cancer drug treatments. However, 40 per cent of all UK health expenditure goes on the over 65s with the costs rising rapidly as people age. Longer survival may mean a longer healthy life, but for the old old (over the age of 75) healthcare expenditures are very high. Care costs are another matter. Decline in family co-location, the pressure on women who often take on caring responsibilities to work in flexible post-industrial capitalism, and the incidence of dementia among the old elderly are all factors driving the need for domiciliary and residential care among the old elderly. In the UK other than Scotland these costs have been met by effective confiscation of the assets of those who possess enough assets and even in Scotland residential care incurs costs, albeit at a lower level. Proposals to deal with this have included advance payments of a social insurance kind which represent a bet on living long and needing care. Whatever mechanisms are adopted, care costs along with health costs are imposing pressures on state budgets. Of course, in most post-industrial states care is very largely a privatised activity generating profits, almost entirely so for residential care and increasingly for domiciliary care at home.

One element which is only implicitly considered in Streeck's account is cultural. If we consider what Williams (1958) described as the 'structure of feeling' of organised working classes, particularly that in the UK after his 'long revolution':

> We may now see what is properly meant by working class culture. It is not proletarian art or council houses or a particular use of language; it is, rather, the basic collective idea and the institutions, manners, habits of thought, and intentions which proceed from this. (p. 313)

Then we have to recognise that this has been massively eroded under the impact of all the economic and political pressures but also by the turn to consumerism as a way of life.

There was a crucial symbiotic relationship between organised working classes and the political parties which emerged from those classes. Sometimes as in the UK and Norway this was explicitly founded in the original central purpose of the parties being to intervene in parliamentary politics in order to ensure that trade unions could function effectively – Labour parties. Whether Labour or Social Democrat or Socialist by name, these parties were founded around a conception of politics as involving a contest of interests between those dependent on wage labour and those who owned the factors of production. The late twentieth century has seen a separation of socialist and labour parties from the organised working classes which created them with a turn, especially marked in the UK, towards being parties of a unitary and uncontested national interest. Mair pertinently describes this in terms of the transformation of political parties away from being collective actors representing social interests:

Contemporary changes in the form of party politics may be specified under two broad headings: the *location* of the parties, and their *political identity*. As far as location is concerned, the past few decades have witnessed a gradual but inexorable withdrawal of the party leaderships from the realm of civil society into that of government and the state. The same period has also seen the steady erosion of the parties' political identities, and the blurring of inter-party boundaries. Together, these parallel developments have led to a situation in which each party tends to become more distant from the voters that it purports to represent, while at the same time becoming more closely associated with the various protagonists against whom it purports to compete. Party–voter distances have been stretched, while party–party differences have lessened; both processes combine to reinforce a growing popular indifference and distrust of parties, and of political institutions more generally...If we conceive of the role and location of parties within a democratic polity as standing somewhere on a spectrum between society and the state, then we can suggest that they have shifted along this continuum from a position in which they were primarily defined as social actors – as in the classic mass-party model – to one where they might now be reasonably defined as state actors. (2006, 45)

All this is part of what Crouch (2000) calls 'post-democracy', a political context in which:

while elections exist and can change governments, public electoral debate is a tightly controlled spectacle, managed by rival teams of professionals expert in techniques of persuasion, and considering a small range of issues selected by those teams. The mass of citizens plays a passive, quiescent, even apathetic part, responding only to the signals given to them. Behind this spectacle of the electoral game politics is really shaped in private by interaction between elected governments and elites which overwhelmingly represent business interests. (2000, 2)

What we have to recognise is the extent to which the causes of the emergence of the consolidation state while certainly being multiple, complex and interactively recursive, have as almost a control parameter the cultural change which allowed Labour and socialist parties to become parties of professional politicians lacking even the 'transmission belts' which supposedly connected even Soviet system Communist parties to the masses. The point is that cultural change may usually be incremental and long running, until quantity results in a change of quality but sometimes it happens fast. This is especially the case if what Williams described as a residual culture of feeling, in this context the culture of feeling of the old organised working class, becomes relevant in connection with emergent cultures of feeling. Now we have a culture of feeling of dispossession, particularly on the part of the young, which may turn back to the culture of feeling which underpinned collectivism in the past.

We will conclude this chapter with a brief assessment of the proposals advanced by critics of austerity for resolving the issues it poses for most people in post-industrial industrial capitalist societies. Blyth stands as a representative of those who adopt some form of Keynesian solution involving a rejection of austerity, increased public sector productive expenditure, and a restoration of mass purchasing power in order to fuel growth and thus resolve whatever debt crisis actually occurs. This is against the neoliberal/consolidationist orthodoxy that austerity is necessary to achieve growth, the thesis formerly known as 'crowding out' which argues that state expenditure deprives the private sector of the resources it needs for productive investment. The ability to regurgitate this in a context where capital has turned to the quaternary sector of finance rather than investment in production of real commodities demonstrates the hegemony of the neoliberal argument. From the point of view of taxation these neo-Keynesians are pro-welfare expenditures and pro-redistributive taxation and a crackdown on tax avoidance, although Blyth is appropriately cynical about the prospects for real action there, suggesting that assertions by mainstream politicians about attacks on tax avoidance will lead to very little and serve as a cover for increases in payroll and consumption taxes.

Streeck is not convinced by the prospects for this kind of development but does not really offer an alternative although he does recognise the need for a consideration of whether post-industrial capitalism is corrigible. We have to ask if there is a set of economic and social policies which can bring post-industrial capitalism back as a functioning system for the mass of people in the way that implementation of the programmes of Keynes and Beveridge did for industrial capitalism. Beveridge in his rather neglected but important text *Full Employment in a Free Society* (1944)[8] said that if his and Keynes' proposals did not deliver full employment, at that time the fundamental basis for the effective industrial and political power of organised labour, then market capitalism had no right to continue to exist. Those were the days!

Post-industrial capitalism with its flexible labour markets seems able to deliver a degraded form of full employment for disorganised labour. Much of the employment is in 'poor work' in terms of remuneration and conditions, and the political progamme of organised labour is in retreat among politicians although the upsurge of the membership of the UK Labour Party indicates that it has not disappeared among the politically active. In this context the politics of taxation matters, not least because taxation is fundamental in relation to social inequality. That issue will be the focus of Chapter Four.

Notes

[1] With the word 'determine' understood, as it must always be in any complexity informed discussion, as Williams (1980) specifies, not in the sense of exact specification but rather as prescribing possible limits within the possibility space for a system.

[2] The IEA in common with other UK rightwing think tanks and pressure groups, notably the Tax Payers' Alliance, an astro-turf supposedly grassroots organisation, is opaque in relation to its sources of funding.

[3] Too many politicians in the UK have PPE degrees from Oxford with the Philosophy dominated by the somewhat sterile analytical tradition and the Economics very much adhering to the neoclassical, for which read neoliberal, orthodoxy. We might regard this as a pretty poor education if we are polite in our designation of the first p in the acronym.

[4] Taxes borne are taxes on capital itself, for example, corporation tax and the cost of irrecoverable VAT to the financial sector. Taxes collected are primarily payroll taxes that is, PAYE income tax and national insurance which fall on individual employees.

[5] Given the degree of deindustrialisation outside perhaps Germany, post-industrial states worry less about the accelerator which kicks in as the demand falls for capital goods.

[6] As Kung (1997) points out, this represented to a considerable degree a reconciliation of market ideologies with catholic social teaching and critiques of unregulated capitalism.

[7] Reinforced in academia by the banal dogmas of the neoclassical school which dominated academic Economics as a discipline.

[8] Harold Wilson, later UK Labour Prime Minister, made important contributions to this.

FOUR

Tax and inequality

While there is a substantial literature on economic inequality arising from variations in income and benefits, there has been by comparison very little analysis of the contribution of taxation to shaping and patterning inequality. To examine the link between taxation and inequality, this chapter will first draw on Office for National Statistics (ONS) data to examine how the UK tax system distributes the tax contribution among households in different parts of the income distribution by looking at the impact of particular taxes and of taxes as a whole. We will demonstrate how the operation of the tax system contributes to and patterns inequality. Second, we will examine how the growing share of income accruing to the top 1 per cent of households is inextricably linked to the declining share of national income experienced by the bottom 60 per cent of earners and how the change in the mode of regulation in western capitalism has been accompanied by critical features in the system of taxation which have reinforced growing inequality and particularly the enrichment of the top 1 per cent.

Shaping inequality through personal taxation

Much of the following analysis is based on data which are derived from the ONS series, 'The Effects of Taxes and Benefits on Household Income'. Despite their shortcomings,[1] these data offer the best opportunity available to us to assess the impact of taxation on households in different parts of the income distribution. The analysis is based on all income and taxes which can be attributed to households. Gross household income (GHI) is all income from wages, salaries and self-employment, tax credits (where relevant) plus occupational pensions and cash benefits as well as investment income *before* any taxes are paid. The figures do not include income which is concealed or not disclosed to HMRC and provide no information about tax avoidance and evasion.

Most taxes can be attributed to households but there is no sound methodological basis for attributing taxes on capital such as capital gains tax and inheritance tax or company taxes to households and nor is this information collected through the survey and so they are excluded from the analysis. The taxes covered include direct taxes – income tax, national insurance contributions (NICs), council tax (or local rates) – and VAT and other indirect taxes such as excise duties, stamp duty and the television licence. The reason for including all of these is that a proper appreciation of the tax burden borne by households in different parts of the income distribution is only possible when the focus moves *beyond* income tax to all taxes, even though much political and media debate on tax focuses misleadingly only on income tax. Households are divided into ten equal size groupings (deciles) ranked according to the value of equivalised disposable income. The figures for income and tax reflect the average for that particular decile and reflect ordinary or real values rather than equivalised values. The figures take tax credits, reliefs and rebates into account.

The overall impact of the tax system on households in different parts of the income distribution can be measured in terms of the proportion of gross household income given up by households in all taxes. If we take a snapshot of the incidence of personal taxation and examine its distribution across households of different income levels we find the following for 2014/15, the most recent year for which figures are available (see Table 4.1 and Figure 4.1).

Table 4.1: Percentage of gross household income paid in all taxes in 2014/15, showing average per decile

Decile	1	2	3	4	5	6	7	8	9	10	Average
% GHI paid in all taxes	46.8	31.4	30.4	30.6	31.8	33.4	33.8	34.2	34.4	34.4	34.1

Source: ONS (2016a) 'The Effects of Taxes and Benefits on Household Income, Historical Datasets'.

Figure 4.1: Total taxes paid as a proportion of gross household income by decile for 2014/15

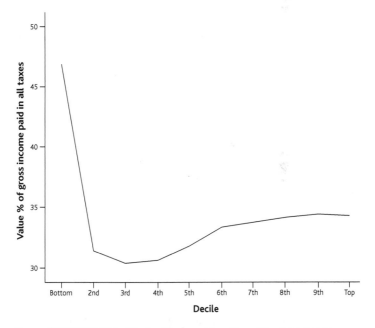

Source: ONS (2016a) 'The Effects of Taxes and Benefits on Household Income, Historical Datasets'.

There are three striking features of this picture. The first is the very high incidence of tax upon the poorest households (the bottom decile). The second is the comparatively modest incidence of tax borne by the best-off households (the top decile or decile 10). And the third is the relatively flat nature of the tax system, once the poorest households are excluded. To understand this we need to consider the impact of the key components of the tax system on households, that is, all of the direct taxes and the overall impact of indirect taxes taken together.

For income tax (net of tax credits), which raised 27 per cent of all tax revenues in 2015/16 see Figure 4.2. This is the most progressive tax in the entire tax system.

Figure 4.2: Income tax paid as a proportion of gross household income by decile in 2014/15

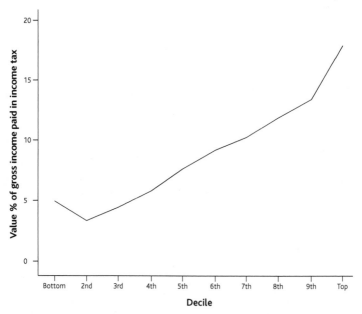

Source: ONS (2016a) 'The Effects of Taxes and Benefits on Household Income, Historical Datasets'.

Figure 4.3: Employees' National Insurance paid as a proportion of gross household income by decile for 2014/15

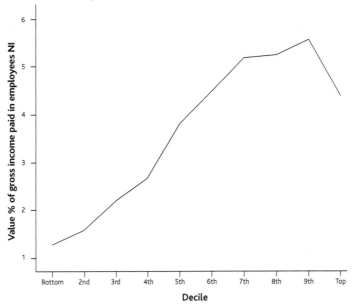

Source: ONS (2016a) 'The Effects of Taxes and Benefits on Household Income, Historical Datasets'.

The second direct tax is national insurance (NI) and the proportion of gross household income paid in employee contributions is found in Figure 4.3. It can be seen that NI is progressive in its impact up until the ninth decile. After that, the tenth decile pays a lower proportion of its household income in national insurance than the seventh to ninth deciles.

The third direct tax is council tax (or 'rates' in Northern Ireland). As can be seen in Figure 4.4, the impact of council tax is regressive – the poorer the household, the higher the proportion of gross income taken in council tax.

Taken together, as seen in Figure 4.5, direct taxes are broadly progressive in their impact although this is weakened by the regressive character of council tax/rates and the partially regressive character of NI.

Figure 4.4: Council Tax paid as a proportion of gross household income by decile for 2014/15

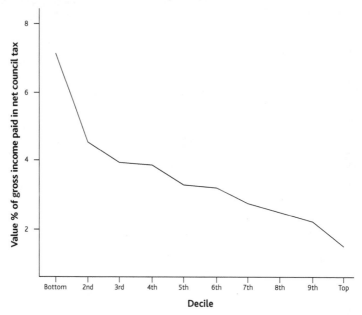

Source: ONS (2016a) 'The Effects of Taxes and Benefits on Household Income, Historical Datasets'.

Indirect taxes include VAT, duties on tobacco, alcohol and fuel, stamp duty on house purchase, insurance premium tax and air passenger duty. Intermediate taxes are levied on goods and services used in the production of final goods and services and include employer national insurance contributions and commercial and industrial rates. All of these taxes are assumed by the Office of National Statistics to be borne by the consumers of the final goods and services (Tonkin, 2015). They are referred to here, generically, as 'indirect taxes'. Almost all indirect taxes are regressive. Figure 4.6 illustrates what happens when all indirect taxes are taken together and measured as a proportion of gross household income.

Figure 4.5: Percentage of gross income taken in all direct taxes 2014/15

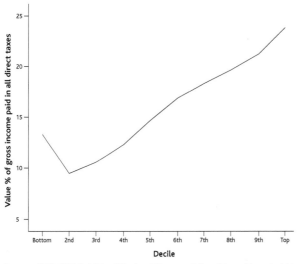

Source: ONS (2016a) 'The Effects of Taxes and Benefits on Household Income, Historical Datasets'.

Figure 4.6: All indirect taxes paid as a proportion of gross household income by decile for 2014/15

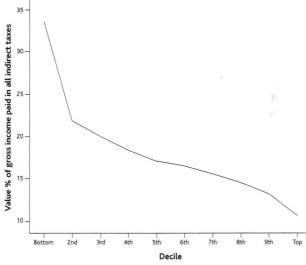

Source: ONS (2016a) 'The Effects of Taxes and Benefits on Household Income, Historical Datasets'.

If we try to explain why the poorest 10 per cent of households bear such a high incidence of tax, we can cite, along with council tax (and rates), the high levels of consumption taxes and VAT they pay. Since these households are likely to be spending from savings or from credit, they bear very high levels of taxes on spending relative to their income. Additionally, a high proportion of their spending is likely to be on goods which are subject to VAT and other duties whereas high income households divert more of their income into activities which incur no VAT or duties such as savings and spending on mortgages. When measured as a proportion of expenditure, the distribution of indirect and intermediate taxes is still regressive, although less so (Tonkin, 2015).

With regard to the relatively low incidence of tax borne by the top 10 per cent of households (even allowing for the exclusion of inheritance tax and capital gains tax which will be disproportionately paid by households in this decile), four factors contribute significantly: the relatively low top rate of income tax, the regressive nature of indirect taxes, the capping of employee national insurance contributions on higher income and the cap on council tax bands with a top band on dwellings set at £320,000. We shall return to these factors later.

Comparing the incidence of tax today with that in the 1970s and the contribution of taxation to inequality

Changes across time in the incidence of tax borne by households across the income distribution can be found in the table below (Table 4.2). The figures cover almost 40 years, from 1977 to 2014/15. The table shows every fifth year plus the most recent year.

There are substantial variations within each decile although the total incidence of tax borne by households has declined substantially across the period as a whole for most deciles and the reduction in the incidence of tax is greatest for the middle deciles. This reduction has not been shared by the bottom (poorest) two deciles which paid a higher rate of tax in 2014/15 than they did in 1977. Setting aside the bottom decile, it is possible to see that the UK tax system has become flatter over time: by 2014/15, all but the bottom decile are paying rates of tax just a few percentage points apart. Right up until and including 2006/7, the top decile gave up a smaller proportion of its gross household income in tax than *most other* deciles. Although not shown in the table above, this was also the case in 2010/11. In 1992, the top decile bore a lower incidence of tax as a proportion of income than all other households.

Table 4.2: Percentage of gross household income paid in (all) taxes by decile and year

Year	Decile 1	2	3	4	5	6	7	8	9	10
1977	42.0	30.8	35.7	38.5	38.5	39.4	39.6	39.5	38.5	36.5
1982	40.2	32.9	35.3	37.6	39.7	40.4	41.5	41.3	40.6	37.3
1987	40.4	32.4	34.6	36.4	38.4	38.8	38.6	38.8	38.7	35.4
1992	46.4	33.8	35.8	38.1	38.3	39.4	39.1	38.6	37.8	33.2
1996/7	43.2	31.7	33.8	35.2	35.9	37.2	37.2	37.2	37.0	34.1
2001/2	53.0	34.6	32.5	34.4	35.9	36.3	37.1	36.3	36.1	33.7
2006/7	47.0	33.1	32.3	33.2	34.2	35.6	36.8	36.6	36.1	34.1
2011/12	43.1	32.3	30.5	31.4	33.3	33.0	34.7	35.1	36.0	35.2
2014/15	46.8	31.4	30.4	30.6	31.8	33.4	33.8	34.2	34.4	34.4
Difference in rate of tax between 77 and 14/15 in % points	+4.8	+0.6	-5.3	-7.9	-6.7	-6.0	-5.8	-5.3	-4.1	-2.1

Source: ONS (2016a) 'The Effects of Taxes and Benefits on Household Income, Historical Datasets'.

The progressive effect of direct taxes as a whole is more than cancelled out by the regressive nature of indirect taxes. Direct taxes were able to nullify the regressive impact of indirect taxes until the mid-1980s but since then the regressive impact of the latter has outweighed the progressive effect of the former (Anyaegbu, 2011). In the period between 1980 and 2009/10, direct taxes reduced inequality by around

3 percentage points but indirect taxes increased inequality by about 4 percentage points as measured by the Gini coefficient (Anyaegbu, 2011). (For comparison, cash benefits reduce inequality by around 15 percentage points.)

Although there is an appreciable increase in the gross household income of the tenth decile when compared with the ninth (and greater than any other income rises between deciles lower down the distribution ladder), the total tax rate paid is in fact slightly smaller for the tenth decile than for the ninth. (This cannot be seen in Table 4.2 but the figures are 34.37 per cent and 34.43 per cent.) Even though income tax is progressive, it does not increase in line with the income difference between the ninth and tenth deciles. Although gross household income between the ninth and tenth deciles leaps by 73 per cent (in 2014/15), income tax paid increases by just 34 per cent (or by 4.5 percentage points). The ninth decile (average gross household income of around £63,500 in 2014/15) has borne a higher incidence of tax than the tenth (average gross household income of around £110,000 in 2014/15) throughout the period.

Indeed, the best off tenth of households has been 'pulling away' from all other deciles, including the ninth decile, in terms of gross household income. In 1977, the top tenth of households held 20 per cent of all gross household income; in 2014/15, it held just under 27 per cent. The higher proportion of all income tax which is paid by the tenth decile simply reflects its growing share of total household income. The tax system, while raising additional revenues from these higher incomes, does almost nothing to counter the growing income gap between the top tenth of households and all other households as evidenced in the exceptionally high post-tax income for this group. As shown in Table 4.3 later, fiscal policy as a whole, including taxes, cash benefits and benefits in kind, creates a more unequal outcome than was the case in 1977.

As the size of the gross household income secured by the top decile has pulled away from that of all other deciles, the tax system has not substantially modified the outcome. Figure 4.7 shows how the gains in both gross and post-tax income by the top 10 per cent have been made at the expense of most other deciles. Particular features of the tax system have had the effect of protecting the income of the best off 10 per cent of households and allowing inequality to grow.

Figure 4.7: Proportion of gross household income and post-tax household income received by decile in 1977 and 2014/15

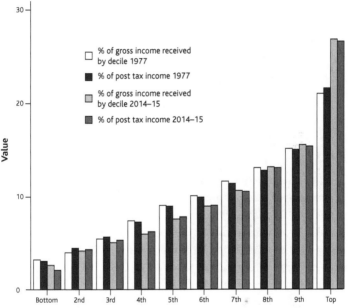

Source: ONS (2016a) 'The Effects of Taxes and Benefits on Household Income, Historical Datasets'.

First the rates of income tax levied on high incomes are modest with, generally, a top rate of tax of 40 per cent in place since the late 1980s. Prior to this, higher rates, up to a rate of 83 per cent for very high incomes, had been reduced from the late 1970s onwards. Second, national insurance contributions, because of their historical connection to defined benefits, a connection now much diluted, are levied in a way which gives financial advantage to those with higher incomes. NICs originate in 1911 and 1912 legislation which established a connection between defined contributions and defined benefits. They provided for horizontal redistribution within the working class, initially excluding the more affluent, and were not extended to cover the whole working population until 1946. Because of this, between 1946 and 2003 no income above the upper earnings limit was subjected to NICs. At the same time, the post-war period saw the introduction of a range of cash benefits and services (including the health service) access to which was not tied to contributions. Thus, NICs neither offer a straightforward link between defined contribution and defined benefit nor a rationally designed form of taxation. Higher rates (currently 12 per cent) are levied on incomes between £112 and £827 weekly (approximately £8,000 and £43,000 per year) in 2016/17 while only 2 per cent is levied on income above that.

Third, council tax and rates are regressive, partly because the top band kicks in for property valued at £320,000 or more with no additional rates for those owning properties well above that value and property values have not been revalued for the purposes of the tax since 1992. This again confers a particular benefit upon those high-income households most likely to own high value property, since they will pay the same tax on property valued well above £320,000 as those whose properties just qualify for the top band.

The peculiar nature of these direct taxes contributes to their inability to counteract the regressive impact of indirect taxes and creates the paradoxical situation whereby the best-off tenth of households pay a lower rate of tax than *some* other deciles and in most years since 1977 and as recently as 2010/11 paid a lower rate of tax than *most* other households. In addition to these provisions is the weak enforcement of the tax rules by HMRC and the vast array of tax avoidance schemes available to, and by accountancy firms actively sold to the affluent. This is not to say that fiscal policies cannot make a difference but rather to observe that the tax system functions as a whole with the effect of preserving the financial advantage enjoyed by those in households with the highest incomes.

Taxation and inequality: the respective contributions of taxation and cash and in-kind benefits

Household income is shaped by a number of processes. First original income is that income derived from wages and salaries, pensions and savings or investments which give rise to an income stream. Cash benefits (and tax credits) are added to give gross income. The deduction of taxes (including taxes on income, property and spending but taking into account tax credits and tax reliefs) gives post-tax income. Finally, the allocation of in-kind benefits (services) to households through spending on services such as education and health gives final income. The ONS data contained in the analyses of the effects of taxes and benefits on household income take into consideration most of the relevant taxes and some services and subsidies.

Table 4.3 shows that inequalities are greater at every stage of the process now in comparison with 1977. The reductions in inequality between original income and final income are achieved through cash benefits and through benefits in kind but not through taxation itself. The tax system itself does not directly reduce inequality – in fact the opposite has been the case since differences in post-tax income are greater than differences in (pre-tax) gross household income. That is to say, some of the redistribution achieved through the allocation of cash benefits is reversed by the tax system. (Of course, the tax system always contributes to redistribution in the sense that it provides the revenues for distributing as cash benefits and for funding services.)

Table 4.3: Ratio of income of top decile to income of bottom decile, including some benefits in kind for selected years

Income	1977	1990/1	2006/7	2014/15
Original income	17.6	41.3	29.4	24.1
Gross income	6.5	10.6	11.5	10.3
Post-tax income	7.2	13.5	14.3	12.7
Final income	4.2	6.6	5.7	6.0

Source: ONS (2016a) 'The Effects of Taxes and Benefits on Household Income, Historical Datasets'.

Spending on benefits and services is progressive. Cash benefits have an obvious financial value but the value of services can also be calculated in cash terms and seen as part of a household's income. Spending on benefits reduces inequality between the original income and gross income stages when assessing the impact of taxes and benefits on household income; spending on services reduces inequality between the post-tax income and final income stages. Note, however, that only certain services and subsidies are included in the ONS *Effects of Taxes and Benefits on Household Income* data (Tonkin, 2015).

Horton and Reed (2010) have gone beyond the ONS calculations and developed a model which allows analysts to see for the first time the distribution of public spending by household on a wider range of services than the ONS considers, taking into consideration how often households used services. They use data from several household surveys concerning which households use different types of services and combine this with data from HM Treasury's *Public Expenditure Statistical Analyses* dataset. Spending in which it is difficult to attribute differential household use (for example, defence) was allocated on a flat rate basis.[2] For all categories of public spending, Horton and Reed found that the value of the spending as a share of net income is greater in lower income households than in higher income households. This matters because while spending on services reduces inequality, by the same token, cuts in public spending on services – as seen in successive budgets since 2010 – have a regressive effect. While higher income households benefit more from tax cuts, they suffer least (as a proportion of their household income) from cuts in public spending on services – these represent a much greater loss to poorer households. For instance, in their analysis of the June 2010 budget, Horton and Reed found the combined changes in taxes, cash benefits and spending on services led to the poorest tenth of households suffering a 23.5 per cent reduction in the value of their household income and the best-off tenth of households losing a much smaller 6 per cent of their income (Figure 4.8). Most middle- and low-income households suffered a greater loss as a proportion of net household income than the richest 10 per cent of households. This points to the regressive character of fiscal austerity which is spending-cut led and to the fact that analyses of the distributional impact of tough fiscal measures underestimate their regressive impact when they omit to quantify the value of spending on services.

Figure 4.8: Distributional impact of all fiscal consolidation measures

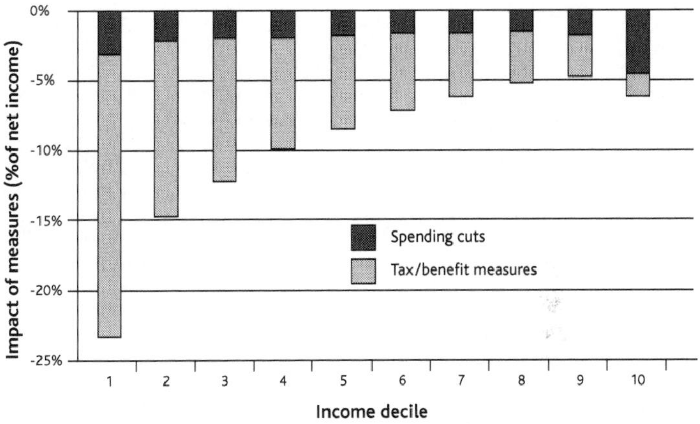

Source: Horton and Reed (2010)

The 1 per cent, the falling wage share of national income and the shifting tax burden

The analysis so far has focused largely on deciles but this conceals inequality within the top 10 per cent and disguises developments at either end of the income scale. While income inequality has declined since the financial crash for the middle 80 per cent of households (Belfield et al, 2016), the trends at the extreme ends of the income scale reveal a dramatically different picture. The top 1 or 2 per cent of households have benefited disproportionately since the late 1970s both from changes in the distribution of market incomes (gross wages, income from self-employment, capital income and returns from savings taken together) and from the way in which the tax system has evolved. Calculations as to the percentage of income accruing to the top 1 per cent vary according to the data set and methodology used. The top 1 per cent of income tax-paying individuals earned on average £159,000 in 2013/14 before tax and £107,000 after tax, according to HMRC's Survey of Personal Income (HMRC, 2016a, Table 3.1a). This amounted to 5.65 per cent of all declared income before tax (up from 5.37 per cent in 1999/2000) and 4.47 per cent of all income after tax (HMRC, 2016a, Table 3.1a). The top 5 per cent held over 18 per cent of all income (again in 2013/14). However, these data are based on a sample of administrative data relating to those liable to pay (income) taxation in the UK and do not include undisclosed income. The Institute for Fiscal Studies (IFS), using household survey data, gives the share of income for the top 1 per cent of *households* in 2014/15 as 7.9 per cent, up from 5.7 per cent in 1990 (Belfield et al, 2016) and the Wealth and Income Database, on the basis of a combination of data sources, gives of the top 1 per cent of *individuals'* share of fiscal income as 12.7 per cent in 2012 (WID, 2016) while Lansley found the top 1 per cent of households held 15.5 per cent of income in 2008 (cited by Lansley and Reed, 2013).

Ruiz and Woloszko (2015) examine in detail technical difficulties involved in measuring the incomes of the most affluent households (and, consequently, the real scale of inequality). They adjust existing approaches to produce a new estimate for OECD countries. Under this measure, out of 34 OECD countries, the UK is the twelfth for highest share of income held by the top 1 per cent; of the European countries in the OECD, it is fifth highest. Table 4.4 shows a comparison with the Wealth and Income Database.

What is clear from all the measures is that the share accruing to the top 1 per cent increased over many years.

The IFS emphasises that there is enormous inequality *within* the top 1 per cent. For example, in 2012–13, of the gross (pre-tax) income flowing to the top 1 per cent of adults, over a third flowed to the top 0.1 per cent (Belfield et al, 2016). Lansley found that while the top 1 per cent held 15.5 per cent of income in 2008, the top 0.5 per cent held 11.5 per cent and the top 0.1 per cent held 6 per cent of income. According to data from Barclays Bank, 1 in 65 adults in the UK was

Table 4.4: Percentage of fiscal income held by top 1% by country and by different data sources

Country	Year	% of fiscal income held by Top 1% WID	Adjusted estimate by Ruiz and Woloszko (2016) following analysis of both IDD and WTID for around 2010 (%)
UK	2012	12.7	8
Germany	2011	13.0	6
France	2013	7.9	6
Denmark	2010	6.4	5
Australia	2013	9.0	9
US	2015	22.0	14

Source: Ruiz and Woloszko (2015); Wealth and Income Database (2016).

a (sterling) millionaire in the UK in 2015 – around 715,000 in total and over 40 per cent more than there were in 2010 (Collinson, 2015).

The measurement of wealth is also fraught with difficulty and, as sufficient data are not collected, there are substantial problems with all existing approaches in the UK (Alvaredo et al, 2016). However, the data from estates we have indicates that the top 1 per cent of households in the UK own between one fifth and one quarter of total personal wealth, showing that wealth is about twice as concentrated as income for the top 1 per cent and about one and a half times as concentrated for the top 10 per cent. The picture from the Wealth and Asset Survey (WAS) is different indicating much smaller shares of wealth held by the top 1 per cent and top 10 per cent (14 per cent and 43 per cent, respectively, when excluding pension wealth and just 11 per cent for the top 1 per cent when pension wealth is included). However, when data from the Forbes Rich List is combined with WAS data to fit a 'Pareto upper tail' (the highest ranked WAS household has notably less wealth than the least wealthy individuals of the Forbes Rich list), an outcome emerges which is much closer to the findings based on the estates data results, though it must be remembered that the survey-based estimates relate to households not individuals. All three approaches to measurement appear to point to an increase in wealth concentration in recent years (Alvaredo et al,

2016). The widespread nature of owner-occupation in the UK has helped reduce the concentration of wealth when compared with other countries which have lower income inequality.

So, perhaps unsurprisingly given the figures above, in the UK, the top 1 per cent was 'racing away' (Belfield et al, 2016) from others in the income distribution at least until the Great Recession. The High Pay Centre (2016) reported that where in 2000 the top executives in the FTSE 100 earned 47 times the average wage of their employees, by 2015 this had risen to 147 times with an average FTSE CEO annual income of £5.5 million. The ratio of FTSE 100 CEO pay to the median full-time worker across the whole UK economy was 183:1 in 2014 (High Pay Centre, 2016).

How have those on the highest incomes been able to benefit so conspicuously? The answer to this explains Danny Dorling's (2015) observation that the richest 1 per cent is no longer as diverse a collection of individuals as it used to be when it would include most public sector higher professionals such as doctors and head teachers. Instead, those who have benefited from financialisation, especially financiers, managers accountants and lawyers, dominate the group.

One part of the explanation lies in the notable increase in the share of the national income which is given in profits. Reed and Mohun Himmelweit (2012) and Lansley and Reed (2013) have analysed historical changes in the 'profit share' and 'wage share' (the proportion of national income paid out in wages) of national income. The latter has declined substantially since 1980 while the former has risen – from around 24 per cent in 1980 to around 27 per cent in 2008, with a disproportionate rise in the financial sector. This has been at the expense of the majority of UK workers and has implications both for the level of inequality and for economic performance.

The wage share of national income has fallen from 59.2 per cent in 1980 to 53.7 per cent in 2011, according to ONS data – a 'wage gap' of 5.5 per cent (OECD data give different values but show the same decline) (Lansley and Reed, 2013). While in the post-war period until the early 1970s, real living standards rose broadly in line with prosperity (and were even slightly higher for low-income and medium-income households) from 1980 till the early 2000s, median income lagged behind, rising by only about 70 per cent of economic growth and inequality grew, with those on low incomes falling further behind. In the five years before the 2008 financial crash, median household incomes stagnated despite economic growth of 11 per cent. Moreover, the falling wage share has not been evenly distributed across the earnings range but has been borne in the UK almost entirely by middle- and lower-paid employees – the bottom 60 per cent of earners in the UK. This has occurred in several rich countries but is particularly striking in the UK (Lansley and Reed, 2013), with the wage fall in the UK significantly greater than the OECD average (Lansley, 2016). See Table 4.5.

Table 4.5: The wage share 1970 and 2007 for selected countries

Country	1970	2007
Denmark	59	65
France	56	57
Germany	59	55
UK	65	60
US	64	60

Source: Reed and Mohun Himmelweit, 2012; based on OECD data as presented by Bailey et al (2011)

The decline in the wage share reflects both the decline in the number of well-paid working-class jobs and the limited wage rises experienced across a range of occupations, on the one hand and, on the other, by the siphoning off of a greater share of the national income by the richest – especially the top 1 per cent and especially through the activities of the financial sector. Several researchers (including Bell and Van Reenen, 2010; Lansley and Reed, 2013) find that financialisation – the growing role of financial institutions in the economy and the restructuring of the productive economy around financial priorities – is the key driver of income concentration. Although this is experienced across many rich economies, it is acutely felt in the UK where a weakly regulated financial sector is dominant, accounting for around 15 per cent of all profits between 2008 and 2010, up from 1 per cent in the 1950s and 1960s (Reed and Mohun Himmelweit, 2012).

The declining wage share is therefore one side of the coin where the rising share of income accruing to the top 1 per cent or 5 per cent is the other. The enjoyment of profits is concentrated among the richest and a number of practices have served to boost the incomes and wealth of the most affluent. Instead of investment in economic growth or higher wages and better terms and conditions for employees, profits and the incomes derived from them have been used to restructure business through large-scale mergers and buy-outs (often on a highly leveraged basis), enriching those who mastermind them; on financial products and speculation; and on the purchase of assets, resulting in inflation in asset prices (Sayer, 2016). Financialisation entailed a shift away from investment focused on organising the production of useful objects and services towards the use of money to make more money regardless of whether the 'investment' would result in useful products or services. This shaped the productive sector as well as the financial sector as those controlling capital investment did not spend it on upskilling and improving the pay of workers or on new equipment for increased productivity in the long-term but instead expanded their financial divisions and focused on activities which would yield interest, extract rent or skim value. The emphasis on quick financial return reflected and shaped the development of a 'shareholder movement' which pushed for the privileging of share value and dividend payments and, increasingly, firms in the productive sector sought to generate revenue and profits by bearing down on costs through sweating assets, reducing pay and conditions (if necessary transferring production to other countries with cheaper labour and weaker regulation), speculating on price differences and engaging in elaborate methods to reduce their tax liabilities (Sayer, 2016). The pay packages (or 'compensation' packages) of those running these organisations in both the financial and productive sectors were supposedly dependent on their effectiveness in generating these revenues and were (and are) designed in a way directly to reinforce these activities. Thus the enrichment of the few, the increasing impoverishment of the many and the growing inequality between them are inextricably interlinked.

Lansley and Reed demonstrate that, while one of the justifications for growing inequality and the rising incomes of the rich is that they facilitate greater investment in the economy, boosting economic performance, the evidence suggests otherwise. They state that:

> the rise in the profit share has not been associated with an improved economic performance in the UK. A study of the comparative economic record of the post-war era and the post-1980s shows that on all counts bar one – that of reducing inflation – the post-war period was superior. Growth and productivity rates have been growing at two-thirds of the average rate achieved in the 1950s and 1960s. Unemployment has been consistently higher. Recessions have become deeper and longer (Lansley, 2011, ch 6). (Lansley and Reed, 2013, 16)

Part of the problem arises from the lack of investment in terms of both gross fixed capital formation and research and development spending which have been, on average lower since 1980 than in the immediate post-war decades. Thus:

> While the profit share increased from around 25 per cent in the 1950s and 1960s to around 30 per cent of GDP from 1980, gross fixed capital formation fell from around 20 per cent to 15 per cent over the same period. (Lansley and Reed, 2013, 17)

Similarly, business spending on research and development has been falling as a proportion of GDP since the 1980s, below that of all the comparator countries mentioned above, while the proportion of the national income accrued in profits has been rising (Lansley and Reed, 2013). The lack of investment, research and development has contributed to low productivity levels in the UK, lower than those in comparable countries (OECD, 2016).

A number of policies pursued by successive governments since the 1980s – and before and since the 2008 crash – have served to boost the share of income taken by the most affluent. Utterly inadequate regulation of the financial sector permitted the evolution of institutional structures and processes which ultimately helped destabilise the whole financial system, leading to global economic contraction and, in the UK and elsewhere, the transfer of banking debts from private banks to the taxpayer. Lansley (2016) describes the policy framework since the financial crash as 'pro-rich and anti-poor' and one of 'reverse redistribution'. Lansley includes in this the use of quantitative easing combined with low interest rates which have inflated asset prices further. Since 5 per cent of individuals hold 40 per cent of all assets, this is a policy which has disproportionately benefited the very wealthy. Knock-on effects have included the growing difficulty for the young and those on middle and low incomes in securing housing with a growing proportion renting where previously they would have taken on a mortgage.

Financialisation is one element of a fundamental change in the way in which capitalism operates, away from 'managed capitalism' in the post-war decades to a more deregulated model which gives more freedom to markets, facilitates a flexible labour force and reduces the role of trade unions. Trade unions help reduce inequality by playing a particular role in raising the pay of middle and low earners. The wage premium (the percentage difference in average hourly earnings of union members compared with non-members) persists for unionised workers (especially in the public sector) although it has been declining. Moreover, a strong trade union presence can have a more generalised effect on workplace practices and expectations. Mishel et al (2012, 4) concluded that 'declining unionization accounted for about a third of the growth of male wage inequality and a fifth of the growth of female wage inequality between 1973 and 2007. Further, unions provide a political check on excessive managerial pay.'

The decline in trade union membership has been much more pronounced in some countries than in others. Lansley and Reed (2013) report that out of 27 European Union countries, only six have a lower trade union density than the UK. In 2015, just 27.9 per cent of all employees had pay which was covered by collective bargaining – 60.7 per cent of public sector employees but only 16.1 per cent of private sector employees (DBIS, 2016) – down from an OECD estimate of 47 per cent in 1990 (OECD, no date) (see Table 4.6). Again, the contrast with other developed countries is startling and note how the figures demonstrate that strong trade unionism is compatible with economic growth.

Table 4.6: Percentage of workers covered by collective bargaining by country

Country	1990 (OECD) (%)	2007 (ILO) (%)
UK	47	28
Austria	98	98
France	92 (1985)	98
Germany	90 (1992)	57 (2013)
Sweden	83	83
US	18	12

Source: OECD (nd); ILO (2015)

In the UK, trade union membership has declined from 13 million members in 1979 to 6.5 million or 24.7 per cent of all employees by 2015 (BIS, 2016). It is very unevenly distributed across the workforce with 54.8 per cent of public sector employees in a trade union, in contrast to 13.9 per cent in the private sector. Employees who are women, in large workplaces (over 50 staff), in full-time work, in permanent jobs or with degree level education are all more likely to be in a trade union than male employees, those in small workplaces, in part-time or temporary work or with no formal qualifications, although in all cases they are fewer than one third of all employees in that category (BIS, 2016).

In a flexible labour market, more employees find themselves in low paid, insecure work, with reduced social protection (for example, against sickness) and weaker pension arrangements. The decline in wages has left more workers on low pay – 21 per cent of the workforce today compared with 12 per cent in the 1970s, the second highest rate of low pay among rich nations (Lansley, 2016). The Resolution Foundation reports that, of the 1.5 million net new jobs added to the UK economy between 2008 and 2015, 46 per cent were self-employed and 30 per cent were part-time (Corlett et al, 2016). Many new jobs are temporary and low paid and come with flexible contracts such as zero-hours contracts.

The connection between the rising share of the top 1 per cent and systems of taxation

Not only has the decline of trade unions reinforced the tendency of the wage share of national income to fall and weakened the checks on top management pay, it has also decisively weakened one of the forces in favour of progressive taxes. There is a clear association between high trade union density (and high levels of employees covered by collective bargaining) and tax revenues as a high proportion of GDP and these are both negatively correlated with inequality. This is to say, broadly, that countries in which total tax revenues are a relatively high proportion of GDP tend to be countries which have a relatively low degree of inequality and countries where tax revenues are a relatively high proportion of GDP tend to be countries in which there is strong trade union membership and collective bargaining coverage. See Figures 4.9 and 4.10.

According to these data, the UK, with a Gini coefficient of 0.358 and tax revenues of 32.9 per cent as a percentage of GDP is the seventh most unequal of 34 countries.

Alvaredo and colleagues (2013) examine the top 1 per cent in historical context across a number of countries. They compare the proportion of total income accruing to the top 1 per cent of households with the value of the top rate of tax throughout the twentieth century in several developed countries. They find that in the US and UK high top rates of tax in the post-war period (for example 60 per cent in the US between 1932 and 1980) led to a reduction in the share of income in the top 1 per cent but that since 1980, the share of income accruing to the top 1 per cent increased by 135 per cent. This U shape in the

Figure 4.9: The relationship between trade union density and tax revenues as a proportion of GDP across all OECD countries for 2014

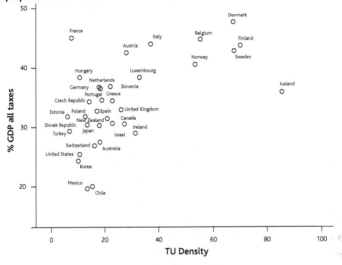

Source: OECD, https://data.oecd.org/economy.htm

Figure 4.10: The relationship between trade union density and levels of within country inequality across all OECD countries

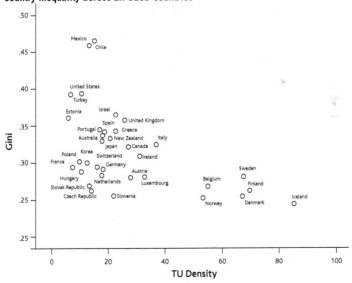

Source: OECD https://data.oecd.org/economy.htm

share of income since the early years of the twentieth century contrasts with an L shape in Germany, France, Japan. In these latter countries, top rates of tax were never as high as the UK's but did reduce the top 1 per cent's share of income and that while the decline has levelled off, there has been no sharp increase in the share of the top 1 per cent in the past 30 or 40 years. Alvaredo et al state that:

> the United States experienced a reduction of 47 percentage points in its top income tax rate and a 10 percentage point increase in its top 1 percent pre-tax income share. By contrast, countries such as Germany, Spain, or Switzerland, which did not experience any significant top rate tax cut, did not show increases in top 1 percent income shares. Hence, the evolution of top tax rates is strongly negatively correlated with changes in pre-tax income concentration.

International contrasts are sharp, reflecting the significance of domestic policy in shaping outcome. In Canada, the income share of the top 1 per cent has increased between 1980 and 2007 by 76 per cent and in New Zealand by 29 per cent (Alvaredo et al, 2013). The authors show a clear association between the share of income held by the top 1 per cent and the level of the top rate of income tax. Atkinson and Leigh (2010) also find that a reduction in the marginal tax rate on wage income is associated with an increase in the share of the top percentile group.

Holding down income tax rates on the richest in society has been decisive for growing inequality and 'centre left' governments have been willing to tolerate growing inequality. Rather than interfering with the 'intensely rich', the New Labour governments of 1997–2010 were more willing to intervene at the lower end of the income spread. During Labour's 13 years in office, redistributive measures included tax credits to those earning low incomes from a weekly minimum number of hours of paid work. These tax credits helped hold up the income growth of those households between the twentieth and thirtieth percentiles and partly counteracted trends towards growing inequality.

Indeed, within the middle 80 percentiles, there was a *reduction* in inequality in disposable incomes (after the operation of the benefit system and direct taxes). However, spending on tax credits and benefits, amounting to some 14 per cent of national income, was insufficient to counteract all the factors contributing to growing inequality. During the period, the poorest 10 per cent of households saw income growth of less than the average, such that the poorer the household, the lower the income growth. Meanwhile the richest 10 per cent saw very strong income growth, and the better off the household, the higher the income growth (by almost 3 per cent annually in the case of the richest 1 per cent) (Johnson and Sibieta, 2011). While median income grew by 23 per cent during the period and mean income by 28 per cent, the incomes of those at the ninety-ninth percentile grew by 56 per cent! While in 1979 a household on the ninety-ninth percentile had an income of three times that of the median household, this had risen to 5.6 times by 2009/10. In 2009/10 alone, the incomes of the top 1 per cent rose by 13 per cent (Johnson and Sibieta, 2011). Thus, net tax revenues were reduced by public subsidy to low-wage paying organisations and inequality increased because the top 1 per cent took a rising share of income partly as a result of the low wages paid to workers.

The most recent analysis by the IFS of UK household inequality finds that while mean income has reached its pre-recession level (2007/08) and median income has exceeded it, average gross employment income across the whole population was still, in 2014/15, lower than prior to the recession (Belfield et al, 2016) but these developments have not been not evenly distributed. Since the Great Recession, those aged over 60 have consistently done better than other age groups while the median income for those between 22 and 30 years of age was still below that of 2007/8. The drop in inequality for the middle 80 percentiles is accounted for by the 'catching-up' of pensioners, by the drop in the level of wages relative to benefits and by the increased importance of employment income in poorer households, with a decline in the number of (non-pensioner) workless households following the Great Recessions (in contrast to earlier recessions) so that as earnings rise they raise the income of households across the spectrum where previously lagging benefits would have held back the income of poorer households.

The IFS analysis confirms the persisting role of the top 1 per cent in detracting from trends towards lower inequality elsewhere in the income spread. Inequality has declined to its level in 1990 with the 90:10 ratio increasing from 3.1 to 4.4 between 1979 and 1990 and has now fallen back to 3.9 (still substantially higher than its 1979 level). The share of income going to the top 1 per cent has risen from 3.3 in 1979 to 5.7 per cent in 1990 to 7.9 per cent in 2014/15 (though it peaked in 2009/10 at 8.7 per cent). Thus, while growing inequality characterised the *whole* of the income distribution in the 1980s, in more recent years it is found at the *top* end of the scale (Belfield et al, 2016). Again, the IFS methodology, vis-à-vis the survey-derived data upon which their analysis rests, systematically understates incomes in the richest households – and consequently the concentration of income in the richest households (see Burkhauser et al, 2016). Additionally, the analysis is based on disposable income and so it does not account for the growing inequality caused by cuts in expenditure on public services, although, as we pointed out above, these are critical to a fuller appreciation of inequality.

Ironically, of course, given the spread of low pay, many of those previously in poverty on benefits are now in poverty while working. The majority of people in poverty are in working households (JRF, 2016) and, according to the IFS, two-thirds of children in poverty are in households where at least one adult works. Belfield et al (2016) state:

> In key respects middle-income families with children now more closely resemble poor families than in the past. Half are now renters rather than owner occupiers and, while poorer families have become less reliant on benefits as employment has risen, middle-income households with children now get 30% of their income from benefits and tax credits, up from 22% 20 years ago.

Changing composition of total tax revenues and shifting the tax burden

There has been a pronounced shift in the tax burden: a higher proportion of total tax revenues are coming from consumption rather than income and from labour rather than capital (Sikka, 2015).

There has been a significant reduction in the proportion of national revenues contributed by personal income taxes (income tax and national insurance contributions) (from 16 per cent in 1978/9 as a percentage of national income to around 15 per cent in 2014/15) although this may recover by 2020/21 while the proportion of total revenues contributed by indirect taxes has increased from just over 8 per cent as a proportion of national income to just under 10 per cent. Equally significant are changes within categories of tax. In relation to personal income taxes, especially income tax and reflecting growing inequality in market incomes, the top 10 per cent and 1 per cent of earners contribute a higher share of total revenues while low paid individuals pay a lower share. The top 1 per cent paid about 11 per cent of income tax revenues in 1978/79 while they now pay around 27 per cent; the top 10 per cent paid 35 per cent of all income taxes in 1978/9 but 59 per cent in 2015/16. The poorest half of tax payers contributed 46 per cent of income tax contributions in 1978/79 but now pay around 31 per cent (Miller and Pope, 2016). Rather than seeing this as an indicator of a fair society, we should note that these shifts reflect the changing fortunes of those groups. As the wage share accruing to the bottom half of earners has fallen, those earning less than around £11,000 (with the tax-free allowance to be increased to £12,500 by 2020–21) are considered too poor to pay income tax. Thus revenue which in the past would have been paid by those earning less than half the median wage has been lost because their wages are now so low. The top 1 per cent are paying more because their incomes have increased substantially. An additional rate and the clawing back of the personal allowance, along with cuts in pension relief for higher earners have also increased tax revenues from them, albeit only in very recent years (Miller and Pope, 2016). The decline in the proportion of adults paying income tax has been marked since shortly before the recession when 65.7 per cent of all adults paid income tax (2007/8) while only 56.2 per cent did by 2015/16 (Miller and Pope, 2016). Within indirect taxes, there has been a noticeable increase in the revenues derived from VAT, especially since the VAT rise in 2011, while the share of tax revenue contributed by excise duties and other indirect taxes has declined, especially through the freezing of fuel duty and the widespread availability of fuel efficient cars, reducing income from vehicle excise duty below what it would have been.

Revenues from corporation taxes (which include onshore and offshore corporation tax, petroleum revenue tax, oil royalties, windfall tax on tobacco companies, the diverted profits tax, bank surcharge and the bank levy) have always fluctuated according to the fortunes of the economy, but overall they are declining. Despite a 65 per cent improvement in overall corporate profitability between 2000/1 and 2011/12, the actual tax take from corporations had declined from £26 billion to £21 billion in that period (Sikka, 2015). At their peak in the mid-1980s, revenues from corporation tax topped 4 per cent of national income but in 2014/15 they had declined to just over 2 per cent. They are set to fall further as a result of declining North Sea oil receipts, a fall in the profitability of banks and cuts in the corporation tax rate (Miller and Pope, 2016). Taxes paid by the financial sector have fallen substantially as a percentage of national income since a peak of almost 0.8 per cent in 20106/7 to around 0.3 per cent in 2014/15. Miller and Pope calculate that changes to corporation tax between 2010 and 2016 have cost almost £11 billion in 2015/16 alone. Further cuts to the rate of corporation tax are planned as the UK seeks to position itself competitively. The decline in corporation tax rates has been evident across the developed world since the 1970s as global competition to attract capital investment has stepped up. Corporation tax was set at 52 per cent of taxable profits in 1982 but dropped to 30 per cent in 2007 and 21 per cent in 2014. We can expect that highly profitable and mobile firms will benefit most from the drop in rates while companies with high levels of investment (or debt) in the UK will benefit least (Miller and Pope, 2016).

Property taxes (on domestic property and business premises) have been a more constant earner of revenues as they do not fluctuate in the same way with wages or economic changes. The UK raises a higher proportion of revenues from property taxes than any other high income country (Houlder, 2016). However, these are due to fall as a proportion of national income in the coming years as permitted additional increases in council taxes levied will not keep pace with economic growth while the tax base for business rates has been reduced through raising the threshold for liability and a more generous relief system (Miller and Pope, 2016). These projected changes pre-date the Brexit vote which has introduced a much higher level of uncertainty.

Despite the dramatically lower levels of corporation tax and top income tax rates when compared with 40 years ago, the National Audit Office reported in 2012 that HMRC was scrutinising over 40,000 tax avoidance schemes (NAO, 2012).

Notes

[1] For details of taxes and sources of income included and for a consideration of the methodology employed in constructing these data, see the relevant methodological publications such as ONS (2016b); Tonkin (2015).

[2] More detail about Horton and Reed's methodology can be found in *Where the money goes: How we benefit from public Services* (2010).

FIVE

The politics of tax and welfare in post-industrial capitalism

Social Democrat/Labour politicians have begun to recognise that the political programme represented by that tradition is in crisis. In exploring the implications of that crisis it is worth reiterating the distinction between the foundational principles of social democratic and labour parties. Labour parties were founded to engage in parliamentary politics in order to defend organised workers against legislative and judicial attacks on the ability of trade unions to strike in order to resist exploitation in the wage/labour relationship. They were parties of waged workers intended to act in the interests of waged workers. Social Democratic parties were founded on Marxist principles to transform capitalist society into something else – a socialist society. They sought to go beyond 'mere' defensive trade union consciousness. This was not necessarily a matter of revolutionary transformation. By the end of the nineteenth century the German Social Democrats (SDP), the prototype party of social democracy, were essentially a reformist movement, albeit one committed in principle to the establishment of a socialist society by reformist means. The old arguments between reformists and revolutionaries have little to say to us now in the context of the complete collapse of any serious revolution-founded alternative to the capitalist social order.[1]

Labour and Social Democratic parties converged in terms of political programmes and forms of action and both can now be described as Social Democrats. They abandoned the objective of a socialist alternative in favour of ameliorating the conditions of social life under capitalism, particularly through policies framed in terms of the Keynes/Beveridge mode of social regulation. They sought to maintain full employment which strengthened the position of workers against employers, developed extensive health and welfare provision, and offered income substitution benefits which provided those not working with a basic minimum income and, in some social insurance systems, with a good deal more than that. Perhaps it was the UK Labour Party in 1945 which actually went furthest in a transformative direction with its extensive, if temporary, nationalisation of 'the commanding heights of the economy'.

No Labour or social democratic party in post-industrial capitalism now has any kind of transformative programme. Most have abandoned even a sustained defence of the model of politics founded around the Keynes/Beveridge mode of regulation. What has replaced this has been a capital-friendly version of a social market economy model as proposed by German politicians with an ordoliberal political programme. The objective became to make capitalism work and resolve its inherent contradictions. The mainstream left seems 'content to appear on the stage of contemporary history as humanisers of the inevitable' (Unger, 2014). We can see this in the 'third way' politics of Giddens (1998), endorsed by Tony Blair and the German SDP Chancellor Gerhardt Schroeder (1999). One of us has described the 'third way' as 'neo-liberalism with a smiley face' (Byrne, 2005). Unger's description of the contemporary state of social democracy is essentially accurate and has been taken up by several centre left politicians in the UK.[2] He differentiates the contemporary global left into recalcitrant and humanising forms. The former seeks to turn back the tide of globalisation and restore something like the Keynes/Beveridge mode of regulation. The latter accepts that there is no way back, regards the hegemony of market relations and globalisation as inevitable, and attempts a programme of amelioration through using tax revenues to transfer income from capital to the rest of society. Note that in Unger's analysis there is no discussion at all of the role of organised labour.

> There is a diametrical connection between the view of the end and the view of the means. On the whole, what happened to the progressives in the closing decades of the 20th century is that they accepted the institutional and ideological settlement of mid-20th-century social democracy as the horizon of their ambitions. They have ever since, for the most part, taken it as their chief work to defend that settlement against the invasions of late-20th-century liberalism. So that means a reluctance to propose any consequential form of institutional change. They present themselves as egalitarians, but when you combine the egalitarian profession of faith with the institutional conservatism, its residual pragmatic significance turns out to be a devotion to compensatory redistribution through tax and transfer. (Unger and Wood, 2014)

This description has been endorsed by the UK MPs John Cruddas and Tristram Hunt[3] and seems entirely accurate in relation to the policy interventions in the UK of Gordon Brown as Chancellor and Prime Minister.

In the era of welfare capitalism much of tax based transfer was actually horizontal. National insurance type systems do not transfer from the owners of property to waged/salaried workers. Rather those who have contingent dependencies from unemployment or illness are funded in terms of income from the payments of those who remain in work. National insurance style pensions are somewhat different but constitute an intergenerational transfer with the retired receiving pensions while those working expect to receive pensions in turn. Given the weak effectiveness of property taxes the only really redistributive tax in most systems is a progressive income tax. In an era of relatively high earned incomes for most workers the taxes of the majority funded the great bulk of benefits and services. Third way style politics attempted to resolve the problem of increasing inequality by redistributive taxation moving resources from very high incomes and the asset wealthy towards low income households. If this had succeeded it would have been genuinely redistributive. However, as we have shown in Chapter Four for the UK example, a great deal of redistribution at the crucial household level was actually within the category of waged/salaried/ pensioned workers and former workers from those in the top half of the income distribution who were not in the top decile or even top 1 per cent to those in the bottom half of the income distribution. Given the ability of owners of wealth and recipients of very high incomes to avoid tax the actual level of redistribution was not high. Gordon Brown as Chancellor engaged in many fatuous policy projects[4] but his belief that UK benefits and welfare provision could be funded from a financial services sector, a large part of which was dedicated to active tax avoidance and whose culture was certainly tax avoiding, was one of his most egregious errors.

What has been the actual role of political parties of the left in the post-industrial era? The historic role of such parties was to act as representatives of workers in a capitalist system. The old Clause Four Part Four of the Labour Party constitution was first about exploitation:

> To secure for the workers by hand or by brain the full fruits of their industry and the most equitable distribution thereof that may be possible upon the basis of the common ownership of the means of production, distribution and exchange, and the best obtainable system of popular administration and control of each industry or service.

This is usually understood as being about the socialisation of the economy and indeed it was, but that was a means to address issues of exploitation which was the fundamental objective of socialist transformation. Even when all notions of general social transformation had been abandoned there was a commitment to representing a class interest. We discussed Mair's (2006) take on this in Chapter

Three and agree with his assertion that the role of political parties in contemporary post-industrial capitalism is to represent the state to the people rather than the people to the state. As Crouch has argued (2000) the predominant interest which mainstream parties including social democratic and Labour parties seek to serve is that of business and corporate capital and they conduct their activities through a language of action which mimics that of business elites.

How does all this relate to issues of taxation and paying for the welfare state? How taxes are raised and how states spend money is central to all political action, but this is not always a central element in political debate, largely because mainstream parties differ only in small matters of degree rather than character about this core element of governance. However, sometimes a political process makes things transparent because fiscal viability can be the key factor in a political dispute. This happened around the Scottish Independence Referendum of 2014 and has continued with the arguments about 'devo-max' and enhancing the fiscal powers of the Scottish government after the failure to achieve independence. With the outcome of the Brexit vote on the UK leaving the European Union, in which a majority in the UK voted to leave but a substantial majority in Scotland voted to stay, the possibility of Scottish independence had resurfaced and again fiscal viability is a core issue.

After the failure of the independence referendum, the Scottish Nationalist Party (SNP) achieved a virtually clean sweep in elections to the UK's national Westminster Parliament in 2015 and, although it lost its absolute majority in the 2016 election to the Holyrood Parliament, it remains by far the largest party and governs alone. Scottish Labour, which since the 1970s had been the hegemonic political force in Scotland, was virtually wiped out at Westminster, being reduced to one seat in the most affluent part of Edinburgh, and in the Holyrood elections came third behind the Scottish Conservatives. It is generally agreed that the SNP achieved this triumph by positioning itself to the left of Labour and presenting as a defender of welfare capitalism and a proponent of civic nationalism. Certainly, it managed to attract the votes of working-class people of Catholic–Irish descent in west central

Scotland, formerly the most solid supporters of Labour and the anti-Scottish Nationalist part of the Scottish electorate.

Scotland had been protected throughout the Blair/Brown years from many of the third way developments which were inflicted on England. Not only had Scotland been very generously treated in terms of public expenditure by the Barnett Formula for the allocation of public expenditure among the devolved nations of the UK, there was no internal market in the Scottish NHS, no development of Academy Schools outwith local government control, and much less general privatisation of services and use of PFI contracts in public sector capital programmes. The SNP is not in any real sense a social democratic party. It is a moderate nationalist party on the lines of Ireland's Fianna Fail or the historic Gaullist tradition in France which seeks to combine friendly relations with business – in Scotland with oil and formerly with the financial services sector – with some mild progressive and welfarist policies. It was not hard to position itself to the left of UK Labour, and the Scottish Labour Party was most incompetently led and marred by small-scale scandals of local corruption.[5]

The SNP is, however, on the horns of a dilemma. It governs Scotland and most welfare/service functions other than cash benefits are under its control as devolved powers. It has significant tax-raising powers in relation to income tax and taxation of land and real property – dwellings and commercial buildings. Although it still receives a greater share of total UK public funding than Scotland would be entitled to on a needs basis, the combination of austerity and redefinition of what constitutes public expenditure, mean that it receives substantially less from the UK exchequer than before the crash and is faced with the prospect of administering austerity on a day-to -basis. Subsequent to the UK Chancellor's Autumn statement of 2016 the Institute for Public Policy Research (IPRR) calculated that:

- Scotland's overall day-to-day budget is due to fall by £800 million between 2016/17 and 2019/20;
- once spending commitments for the NHS and police have been factored, spending on non-protected departments is due to fall by £1.3 billion per year by 2019/20;
- this will leave unprotected departments with budgets which are 11.3 per cent or £1.6 billion lower per year (2016/17 prices) by 2019/20 as compared to the start of this spending period in 2015/16 (excluding how tax revenues perform in Scotland).

In the same week, the economist Anton Muscatelli, in a presentation to the Holyrood Parliament's Finance committee, predicted that Scotland's annual budget from Westminster faces a £3.3 billion contraction from its level of six years ago, with the financial position likely to worsen further after the UK leaves the European Union. Austerity is already biting hard in Scotland and is about to bite even harder.

Arguments around fiscal viability at the time of the Scottish Independence Referendum of 2014 are worth revisiting. Although the SNP was in origin a crude and simplistic nationalist party it managed to position itself slightly to the left of Labour on many issues, although elements in its historic programme – for example reducing the level of Corporation Tax in an independent or even devo-max Scotland – are pro-business rather than pro-labour. The other key factor was the discovery of substantial oil and gas reserves in the Scottish sector of the North Sea. The SNP has long asserted that 'it's Scotland's oil'. If Scotland had had control over oil revenues since their discovery and had invested them, as Norway has, in a sovereign wealth fund, then it would be in a very strong fiscal position. Taxation of oil and gas, which technically is a rent, meant that Scottish tax revenues in total exceeded actual public expenditure in Scotland; so for many years Scotland was a net contributor to the UK exchequer. However, both reductions in oil production and the massive fall in oil prices in recent years mean that the SNP's assertion that it could run a satisfactory expenditure regime with good social provision because oil revenues would bridge the fiscal gap is now incorrect.

Labour campaigned very hard against independence in the referendum on a common platform with the Conservative and Liberal Democrat parties, at that point governing the UK in a coalition which was unpopular in Scotland. A crucial argument presented by this 'Better Together' platform was that an independent Scotland was not fiscally viable if the levels of social provision were to be maintained. The actual pattern of voting in the referendum was very interesting. The Yes campaign did not carry areas in the North East of Scotland, its historic electoral stronghold, but did carry industrial areas which historically supported Labour. Under the leadership of Nicola Sturgeon the SNP has positioned itself as an anti-austerity party and this seems to have been an important factor in its destruction of Scottish Labour. The crucial question is 'Could an independent Scotland with a tax regime on current lines actually deliver the anti-austerity programme which the SNP promises?'

An examination of the anti-independence documents dealing with taxation and welfare in a putatively independent, or even 'devo-max' Scotland, sustains Streeck's account of the character of the consolidation state in terms of the arguments they present. This is particularly the case for the reports of the House of Lords Economic Affairs Committee (2013), a range of publications from the Institute for Fiscal Studies – Adam et al (2013), Johnson and Phillips (2012), Phillips and Tetlow (2013), and the overwhelming majority of commentaries in the UK national press. A key IFS report *Fiscal Sustainability of an Independent Scotland* asserts that:

> the main conclusion of our analysis is that a significant further fiscal tightening would be required in Scotland, on top of that already announced by the UK government, in order to put Scotland's long term public finances on a sustainable footing... Public account net debt in Scotland would rise every year as a share of national income and exceed 100% of national income by 2033–34...Scotland would require a permanent tax increase or spending cut (or combination of the two) equal to 4.1 per cent of Scottish national income (about £6 billion in today's terms)

to be implemented by 2021–22 to put Scottish public sector debt on course to reach 40% of national income by 2062–63. (Amior et al, 2013)

In the short term, the fiscal issues facing Scotland derive from the combination of continued imposition of austerity by Westminster and the implications of the further devolution of taxation powers to Holyrood under the 2015 Scotland Act which implements most but not all of the proposals of the Scott Commission established by the pro-coalition parties to prepare proposals in relation to their promise of greatly increased devolution if the Scottish electorate voted against independence. In present circumstances about 35 per cent of Scottish public expenditure will be funded by taxes collected under devolved powers. The crucial new devolved elements are power over the rates and bands of income tax (although what is important is that there will be no devolved power to charge different rates of tax for different sources of income), air passenger duty, and some assignment of VAT levels. Of an estimated £9.1 billion devolved taxation, £3.5 billion would come from the basic rate of income tax, £0.65 billion from higher rate income tax, £1.9 billion from business rates and £1.8 billion from council tax. These taxes together constitute 86 per cent of potential devolved revenue.

The 2012 Scotland Act had already given Scotland the power to set a Scottish rate of income tax by increasing the first 10 per cent of tax rates but the 2015 act extends this considerably. However, Scotland does not have a large number of very high individual income recipients as less than 1 per cent of Scotland's 2.65 million income tax payers pay the highest additional tax rate on taxable income over £150,000 and 10.6 per cent pay the higher tax rate on taxable income over £31,785.[6] The ability and motivation of additional rate tax payers, the very highest income earners, to avoid tax is considerable.[7] The failure to devolve national insurance contributions to Scotland, the third largest source of UK tax revenues and a significantly regressive tax in its mode of collection, is a crucial omission. In many ways, the devolution of income tax rates and bands to Scotland is a poisoned chalice since without control over national insurance and all consumption taxes the ability of Scotland to create a redistributive tax system is very limited.

Although some benefit powers were devolved under the 2015 Scotland Act, crucial powers over Employment Support Allowance, Job Seekers' Allowance, Pension Credits, Universal Credit and state pensions were not. The only politically salient element will be the continued ability of the Scottish government to attempt to negate the impact of the 'bedroom tax'. This will make it impossible for Scotland to make any serious progress on implementing the positive and redistributive recommendations of the Expert Group on Benefits which reported before the referendum. Not only do they represent a very different take on conditionality from the current UK situation, by rejecting the notion of a benefits cap they have a very different cultural take on benefit recipients from the demonisation engendered by first the coalition and then the current Conservative administrations.

SNP governments have been extremely timid in relation to taxation and did almost nothing which would increase tax revenues prior to the 2015 extension of its powers. Council tax has been frozen by SNP governments since 2007 although the freeze will be lifted in 2017. There has been no revaluation of domestic property since 1991 during which time property values have boomed. The power to add 1p to the basic rate of income tax was never adopted by any devolved Scottish government. The SNP has generally proposed policies which would reduce the tax burden on business arguing for a lower rate of corporation tax, the abolition of air transport related tax, and has given small businesses a substantial reduction in business rate liability. In the autumn of 2016 council tax bands were adjusted which will make the tax slightly less regressive. The Scottish government has used its powers under the 2015 Act to not implement the raising of the threshold for the higher rate of income tax in Scotland. Labour in the Westminster Parliament endorsed this Conservative decision although it affected just 17 per cent of income tax payers. This was represented as a concession to the 'squeezed middle', but an income of £42,866 (which was the effective threshold for the higher rate of tax as of 2015 when the personal allowance was factored in), as the sole income of a household, would put that household in the top 30 per cent of household incomes in that year and the individual in the top 15 per cent of individual incomes. Politicians' use of the term 'middle' seldom refers to any real middle in the structure of inequality.

The reason given by the SNP Holyrood government for not raising the additional highest rate of income tax from 45 per cent to 50 per cent illustrates the problems faced by parties seeking to maintain high levels of tax funded services and welfare in a post-industrial context. This (Scottish Government, 2016) shows that in 2015–16 there were 17,000 additional rate taxpayers in Scotland with an average tax declared income[8] of £310,000 which was lower than the UK average for this group at £370,000. This category represented 0.7 per cent of Scottish income tax payers but delivered 13.7 per cent of income tax revenue.[9] Across the UK the 1.1 per cent of tax payers in this category provide 27.3 per cent of income tax revenue. The document reproduces the usual conservative estimates of the behavioural likelihood for very high income earners to reinforce their tax avoidance if rates are raised.[10] That said, there is no doubt that simple relocation of primary residence in what remains a United Kingdom from Scotland to England would be easy for many of these people. In Scotland, many are public sector employees but these are in the lower bands of very high incomes and as the document points out, relocation of someone earning £1 million would cost the Scottish tax base £440,000 because all income tax would be lost to Scotland. The SNP's commentary states that if just 7 per cent of additional rate tax payers relocated then the loss to the revenue would be £30 million per annum.

Differential tax rates within a single nation state always raise issues of collection. In countries where sub-national tax is an important part of the tax base, there has often been a race to the bottom, particularly in relation to taxes on property and corporation taxes. The SNP's dilemma illustrates the issues facing parties which seek to maintain some form of welfare capitalism during the current economic crisis. Perhaps the high tax, high trade union presence, and still being engaged in advanced manufacturing and/or possessed of oil revenues of Scandinavian states identified in Chapter Four might be able to resolve this without a truly radical programme, but it is difficult to see this happening elsewhere.

The 'radical' alternative which is offered as a solution is generally a reassertion of the Keynesian model. This was well summarised in an article by the UK *Guardian*'s Economics Editor, Larry Elliot: 'A view from 1936: What would Keynes say?' (12 December 2016) and for a fully developed European Union attempt to develop the line see Meyer (2016). The argument is for confronting recession by states running a deficit budget with a focus on investment rather than funding current spending. Given the very low interest rates currently available, as Elliot notes, this would not 'scare the markets'. Indeed, the markets would be keen to buy bonds from governments with a good reputation. The monetary policy of quantitative easing could be reconfigured towards average and lower income households rather than increasing the price of assets held by the wealthy. The investment focus makes considerable sense but Keynes devised his approach for industrial societies and in a post-industrial world increased consumption does not necessarily translate into increased domestic production. It can exacerbate trade imbalances and with the current massive imbalances between the post-industrial west and the new industrial world, especially China, this is a very real problem.

Economic base matters and there is real path dependency which is particularly acute for the UK as a whole, and even more acute for Scotland considered as a separate economic entity. What about the contemporary politics of economic management and particularly the politics of taxation? Bonica et al (2013) offer five reasons in answering the question: 'Why hasn't democracy slowed rising inequality?' Although their paper is focused on the USA, their analysis is readily transferable generally. They argue that:

1. There has been an ideological shift in political parties which involves a retreat from the state as a key economic and social actor and a belief in the optimising potential of free market capitalism. This has resulted in deregulation, particularly in the financial sector, and a reluctance to use taxation as a major redistributive mechanism.

2. Lower electoral turnout by lower income voters biases elections and hence electoral strategies towards the interests of the better off.

3. Rising income and wealth has meant that a large proportion of the population are less committed to general social insurance. Bonica et al note that in the US, while social security to secure higher incomes in old age has become less politically attractive to the middle classes who rely on their own provision, there continues to be mainstream political support for health spending since a catastrophic health episode is a real possibility for middle-income people.

4. The rich, and we would add, following Crouch (2000), corporations, use their wealth to influence the political process. With the lack of restrictions on campaign funding the very short term for members of the House of Representatives this is a particular problem in the USA, but it is true elsewhere. What Attlee or Bevin would have made of the term 'Labour donor' is not very much, but even 'socialist' parties now take money from the super-rich.

5. In the USA, systematic gerrymandering of congressional districts by state governments reduces the accountability of elected officials. We might add that the peculiarities of the US electoral college allow a President to be elected with a minority of the popular vote and the bias is to the right. In the UK, for Westminster elections first past the post allows majority government with the support of a minority of voters and was essential to the Thatcher revolution. Scotland's proportional representation for Holyrood elections has very different implications for executive power.

So the rich always win? Or do they? Pizzigati (2012), in documenting 'the forgotten triumph over plutocracy that created the American middle class', argues that they don't, or perhaps more accurately we must say 'didn't'. Roosevelt's attack on wealth and at least rhetoric (and by present-day standards, reality) of progressive taxation was denounced by his right-wing opponents as communism. He was under considerable pressure from a genuine populism of the left, typified by that complex and interesting figure Huey Long. Increasing unionisation through the development of the CIO which went beyond the skilled labour of the AFL was a major factor in the massive majority FDR obtained in his second election victory. Despite opposition from conservative Supreme Court Justices, eventually workers in the USA won the right to organise, not least through their own industrial action and the insurrectionary threat this posed to the overall social order.

Reagan in the USA, like Thatcher in the UK, began the political roll-back on progressive taxation. In the UK, top rates of income tax dropped from 77 per cent in 1964 to 40 per cent in 2013. The threshold for this highest rate dropped dramatically over these years in real terms, which has had the effect of transferring liability from very high incomes, where there is massive legal tax avoidance, to the top half of the middle-income range. In the UK in the 1970s with a surcharge on investment income, the highest rate of tax was 90 per cent. Currently it is 45 per cent and given that unearned income is not liable for national insurance and that over a ceiling of £43,000 per annum employees pay only 2 per cent on that income, this compares with a real rate of 35 per cent of tax from most employees. Of course, with increasing inequality the highest income recipients have more income and pay tax on those very high incomes, to the extent that they do not avoid that tax. This is the fiscal component of the 'trickle down'[11] strategy which has informed political quiescence in the face of massively growing inequality of incomes.

Plainly the abandonment of any kind of critique of capitalism, even of the kind which informed the liberalism of Beveridge and Keynes, has been a crucial factor in all aspects of the contemporary state of post-industrial industrial societies. The intellectual left, as represented, for example, by the inanities of the offscourings of bourgeois Stalinism who used *Marxism Today* in a fashion which abandoned any of Marx's insights into the fundamental contradictions of capitalism, gave up. This left the ground clear for ideological rantings of the proponents of market capitalism, particularly by think tanks represented in the UK by the Institute of Economic Affairs.[12] The Soviet system had ceased to offer any real kind of alternative to welfare capitalism by the 1960s.[13] Welfare capitalism had worked well, but what has succeeded it is post-welfare capitalism. Inequality has increased massively, most markedly in the UK which has experienced the most dramatic abandonment of the welfare capitalist model, but also elsewhere although to a lesser degree, particularly in the high tax and high union organisation of Scandinavia. If there is to be any chance of a fairer social order in the post-industrial world, then the politics of taxation have to be placed front and centre. The revelations about tax evasion and avoidance which have emerged from the work of Murphy and others in the Tax Justice Network and the leakage of the Panama papers detailing the dirty deeds of the personal tax avoidance industry have made unfairness in the collection of tax a public issue. To move forwards an attack on tax avoidance is the first element in a new system for funding the welfare state but more than that will be required. We need a system of taxation coupled with a restoration of the effectiveness of trade union organisation which fits the character of post-industrial capitalism. The conclusion to this book will make some suggestions about what that programme and set of policies might look like in practice.

Notes

[1] China is now a capitalist society governed by a communist party as is Vietnam and with the somewhat different cases of Cuba and North Korea excepted there is no communist society left in the contemporary world.

[2] The description is useful. Unger's prescriptions for the future are vacuous twaddle which is probably why they appeal to those New Labour politicians with enough intelligence to know that their project is in terminal disarray but are not prepared to start from a class analysis of any kind in attempting to deal with the issues they face.

[3] Hunt has now abandoned politics to scuttle off to be a museum director.

[4] Funding new NHS and other capital developments through private finance initiatives which led to tax revenues being paid to offshored tax entities which paid no UK tax was a prime example of Brown's combination of arrogant disregard of criticism and ignorance of the reality of contemporary finance capital.

[5] Although the SNP has had its own problems, not least with some of the MPs it sent to Westminster.

[6] The 1990s shifting of income tax liability from married couples to individuals has been massively advantageous for high-income households and is a significant source of increasing current and inter-generational inequality.

[7] For details see Berthier, 2014.

[8] This expression should always be used when referring to this group since they engage in large-scale legal tax avoidance.

[9] The table in the document refers to total tax revenues rather than total income tax revenues. This shoddy slippage is characteristic of policy documents on this topic and reinforces the view that income tax is the only tax that matters.

[10] The literature on this topic pays far too little attention to the way in which enforcement, penalties and indeed the criminalisation of various currently legal avoidance strategies can modify this behaviour.

[11] A trickle is a very weak flow indeed. A radical alternative would be at least a stream if not a torrent.

[12] Characteristically the IEA is not transparent about its sources of funding but acts as part of an Anglo-Saxon world of right-wing think tanks funded by the super-rich.

[13] The forcible suppression of 'Socialism with a human face' in Czechoslovakia in 1968 – David Byrne was there and saw it happen – ended the possibility of a realignment of Euro Communism and Social Democracy around any kind of programme of radical reform.

Conclusion

Taxation is part of the overall socio-cultural-economic system which constitutes the social world. To assert that it is part of the socio-economic system is utterly conventional. To add the word 'cultural' to that portmanteau expression is not but we assert that an understanding of the cultural content of taxation is absolutely necessary if we are to have any chance of establishing modes of taxation which can address the fundamental issues which have emerged from the transition of industrial societies to their current post-industrial condition. Table 6.1 summarises key differences between the industrial and post-industrial eras in work and taxation.

Since we are working in the complexity frame of reference (Byrne and Callaghan, 2013) when we say that taxation is part of the overall system we mean not only that it is dependent on the character of that system but that it is a crucial constitutive part of the system with causal powers in relation to the nature of the system as a whole. What is possible in terms of the character of a post-industrial system is therefore circumscribed by the reality of post-industrialism, but the form of the taxation system will play a crucial role in determining the actual form of the post-industrial system itself. The possibility space for a post-industrial taxation system exists within the possibility space for post-industrial societies, but the form of any particular post-industrial society will be a function of its own taxation system. In Table 6.1 we summarise what we see as key differences between the industrial and post-industrial eras.

Table 6.1: Differences in the employment relation and taxation systems of the industrial and post-industrial eras

Industrial employment relations and tax system	Post-industrial employment relations and tax system
Keynesian/Beveridge mode of regulation	Post-industrial/consolidation state mode of regulation
Industrial workforce approaching half of total workforce	Primarily service sector workforce; industrial workforce less than 15% of total
Full employment with frictional unemployment	Disguised unemployment (eg extension of higher education; early retirement); underemployment
Job security and substantial worker rights	Flexible labour – spread of precarious employment, limited worker rights
Employer-borne risk and responsibilities to workforce	Transfer of risk to workers – use of zero hours contracts and forms of self-employment
Large public sector and devalorised labour	Declining public sector as proportion of all employment and recommodification of labour
Relatively high trade union membership	Low trade union membership
Relatively high wages	Lagging wages and spread of low wages; heavy reliance on wage subsidy
Strong protections for workers in public sector	Workers in public sector exposed to market competition
Status and protection for professionals	Extension of Fordism into professional work and proletarianisation
High top rates of income tax	Relatively low top rates of income tax
Relatively strong link between national insurance contributions and benefits received	Weak link between national insurance contributions and benefits received
Higher corporation tax rates	Lower corporation tax rates
Avoidance and evasion practices which do not catastrophically compromise the tax system	Avoidance and evasion practices which catastrophically compromise the tax system
Strong and independent tax collection authorities	Weakened tax collection authorities strongly influenced by corporate lobbying

Both of us are socialists in the tradition of democratic socialism/labourism/free trade unionism. We regard the achievements of the democratic left in establishing the post-Second World War welfare states as the greatest achievement of the socialist project with the British welfare state established in the 1940s as the exemplar of that project of radical reform. For us what has happened to the societies which had managed to modify industrial capitalism towards a much more equal and acceptable social order in those years is a tragedy. And it is a tragedy which had protagonists on stage. The malignant influence of Thatcherism in the UK stands as a key example but Christian Democrats, Social Democrats and Labour Parties have been drawn in the same direction across Europe and Australasia. Wherever they have been in power they have seemed to repeat Unger's assertion that they are content 'to appear on the stage of contemporary history as humanisers of the inevitable' (Unger and Wood, 2014). O'Connor said it all when as we noted in the Introduction he described tax systems as 'simply particular forms of class systems' (O'Connor, 1973; 2002, 206). Since they are forms of class systems they are domains in which class conflicts are conducted and the capitalist class – a collective actor on the stage of history – has been enthusiastically and competently engaged in constructing tax systems which favour itself. The consequence of this has been a massive increase in inequality. This is not just a state. It is a trajectory. Post-industrial capitalism has not just become more unequal. The fundamental tendency is that it will become even more unequal yet.

The most important aspect of the increase in inequality between industrial capitalism and post-industrial capitalism is the relative immiseration of the working class in O'Connor's monopoly sector on the one hand and the radical increase in the incomes and wealth of the very affluent on the other. The terms and conditions which O'Connor described for the competitive sector of capitalism have been imposed on workers in major industrial sectors and on workers in the state sector. In the UK, the introduction of competition and privatisation has been crucial to the immiseration of workers shifted from the state sector, but the reduction in income and conditions is now being applied to directly employed state workers. Austerity with its emphasis on 'efficiency savings' is making this bad situation even worse. There are numerous drivers for this trajectory of ever-increasing inequality. Globalisation, deindustrialisation, the making 'flexible' of the labour market, and the combination in a paraphrase of the words of the Red Flag of 'cowards flinching and traitors sneering' by elected politicians of the left all contribute to it. Taxation systems are key control parameters, especially in combination with benefit systems. The allowing of avoidance as an aspect of the financialisation of post-industrial capitalism with 'tax efficiency' being a key driver of the behaviour of corporations and very affluent individuals and 'the tax avoidance industry' being an ever more important part of the financial sector, plays a crucial role in driving up inequality. If anyone had thought sensibly about the implications of the subsidisation of low/part-time wages from the tax revenues collected in very large part from the Joe Soaps who constitute the bottom 95 per cent of the tax base and avoided so systematically by the 5 per cent who are the top of that tax base, they might have recognised that this was probably the stupidest possible way of trying to reduce social inequality. A high and enforced minimum wage, the outlawing of zero-hours contracts and above all else the restoration of trade unions' ability to engage in effective defensive and even offensive industrial action would have been the way to go, but who in 'New Labour' ever saw that?

The UK stands as a prime example of the ineffectiveness and incompetence of centre-left parties in government. The privatisation agenda not only has resulted in the driving down of low wages and reductions in service levels – the appalling state of the privatised prisons stands as an excellent example – it has been associated with 'financial engineering' which has located the beneficiary owners of the privatised entities offshore and outwith the UK tax base. The continued existence of tax havens is a crucial enabler of both corporate and very wealthy individual tax evasion. In this Conclusion we want to consider what is to be done if we are to use tax systems to redress inequality and fund the necessary services of something which looks like welfare capitalism. If we ask what is to be done, however, we also

CONCLUSION

have to ask what can be done? We are where we are. There is a path
dependency in any complex system and the socio-cultural-economic
system of post-industrial capitalism is in a particular position globally
and the systems of individual nation states are located in particular sub-
sets of the location of that overall system. Change is possible but the
range of possible changes while certainly large, is nonetheless limited.

The taxation of housing in the UK illustrates this very well. In any
rational housing system there would be a tax on the real incomes
owner-occupiers derive from living in the properties which they
own – a Schedule A tax as it existed in the UK up until 1963. This
would be based on a realistic mode of valuing those incomes. The
absence of such a tax not only grossly distorts the housing market itself
and has generated a trajectory of ever increasing house prices but also
has distorted the whole pattern for investment of savings in favour of
housing and away from investment in other domains. It would be very
difficult to reintroduced Schedule A politically since it would impose
a large tax burden on owner-occupiers as a group. It has been difficult
enough to have proper revaluations of domestic property in order to
reform the existing mode of taxation of domestic property – council
tax. This is constantly deferred for reasons of immediate political
expediency. Any proper taxation of owner-occupation would certainly
lead to a fall in house prices, something which has become equivalent
in the UK's overall political mindset to the impact of bubonic plague.

Political contexts themselves change, however. In much of the
UK access to owner-occupation for households seeking it, first-time
buyers, has become virtually impossible for households in the middle
quintiles of the household income distribution. The alternative of
reasonably priced social housing is in extremely limited supply. For
many middle-income owner-occupiers there is a direct personal
connection to those middle-income households forced into renting
because they cannot afford to enter owner-occupation. They contain
their children and grandchildren. Moreover, the whole space economy
of the UK is distorted by the way in which house prices in London
have become so radically separated from the UK norm. It will not
be easy to reform the taxation of UK domestic property, but it is not

impossible because overall system change is opening up new domains in the possibility space. This is happening because young people and their parents experience the failure of the system as it stands. Let us turn to what is more immediately possible and consider what moves are already underway which might facilitate the development of tax systems which could fund welfare states in post-industrial capitalism.

Where now?

The most important source of possibility for tax reform is a change in political culture mediated by the excellent work of critics like the Tax Justice Network who have revealed both the extent of tax dodging by corporations and very wealthy individuals, households and families[1] and the weakness of political responses to this by elected governments and the tax authorities of post-industrial capitalist states. This is particularly true of the UK where HMRC has made sweetheart deals with large corporations and excused even large-scale criminal tax evasion by individuals who have used the Swiss Banking system to conceal taxable income and assets. Scandals, not least the issues surrounding the collapse of British Home Stores and the threat to its pension fund associated with the notorious tax avoider Philip Green (Sir Philip as he was knighted by the Blair government for 'services to retail'), have reinforced a very high degree of public resentment of the reality that the old adage – two things in life are inevitable: death and taxes – no longer applies if you are rich enough; 'you' being either individuals/households or corporations. If as in the words of the US tax evader Leona Helmsley: 'Only the little people pay taxes', then expect resentment when the little people find out that this is how things are.[2] Of course the 'Masters of the Universe' of speculative finance capitalism, the operators at the top of the quaternary mode of accumulation in financialised economies, are both notorious tax avoiders themselves and facilitators of tax avoidance by others. Subsequent to the financial crash they too are vulnerable targets of popular discontent. There is a massive fund of resentment and anger about these issues out there if only politicians would use it to drive systematic redistributive tax reform. Blyth (2013b) in a reply to his critics places great emphasis on the ideological character of the austerity programme. We are perhaps more Marxist than he is these days and assert the importance of the inherent systemic contradictions in post-industrial capitalism, but we agree that ideology matters and the domain of politics is the field of ideological conflict. The UK Labour Party during the years of the Conservative/Liberal Democrat coalition government was pathetically inadequate in conducting any kind of ideological battle in the field of popular political culture. It allowed the coalition parties to maintain the flat lie that the deficit in UK public expenditure was a consequence of over spending by government rather than very largely a result of bailing out the banks during the financial crisis and the collapse of tax receipts during the recession caused by those same banks.

The consequences for the revenue base of post-industrial democracies of systematic tax avoidance is on both domestic and international policy agendas. The most coherent international focus has been on the taxation of corporations in terms of 'base erosion and profit shifting'. International coordination on this is managed by the OECD who published their action plan on this in 2013. We agree with the criticism of this by the UK's All Party Parliamentary Group (APPG) on Responsible Tax (APPG, 2016). It is weak on enforcement of country by country reporting of taxable corporate income – the crucial mechanism in avoiding the shifting of profits from turnover to low tax regimes, and spectacularly inadequate in relation to the regulation and control of tax havens. Here successive British governments have a good deal to answer for. They could easily have used Orders in Council to impose regulation and declaration of beneficial ownership on all British Dependent Territories which include the notorious tax havens of the Isle of Man, the various Channel Islands, the British Virgin Islands, Bermuda and others. They have not done so. The APPG's description of the OECD proposals as amounting to nothing more than 'a sticking plaster' is entirely accurate. In dealing with the taxation of profits from corporations what is required is that taxes are paid in the places where revenues are generated. The appalling irony of Amazon

UK exporting profits while its workers in its UK distribution centres have their inadequate wages subsidised from UK taxes is the kind of scandal which should drive political action on this issue.

The tax avoidance of multi-nationals is conservatively estimated by the OECD to rob national exchequers of some $100 to $240 billion per annum. Tax Justice Network[3] considers that a more reliable figure is a revenue loss of $650 billion with $400 billion of this coming from OECD countries. But this is not the total of corporate tax avoidance. The use of limited companies as tax avoiding devices by people who would otherwise be directly employed, not least by prominent figures in the news and commentary areas of the broadcast media, matters. There is no liability for national insurance and corporation tax is now lower than the basic rate of income tax. This amounts to less than the avoidance by transnationals but it is not trivial and certainly no one employed directly from a tax revenue, for example from the television licence fee, should ever be paid on this basis.

The other crucial components of the tax base are taxes on consumption, taxes on incomes, taxes on wealth, and taxes on real property[4] – both domestic and commercial. If we want more equality then the bias in these elements must, wherever possible, be progressive. This is very hard if not impossible to do for taxes on consumption but it can be done relatively easily for taxes on income, wealth and real property. There are two kinds of taxes on income – income taxes and social insurance payments. In the UK, there is no longer any real distinction between these because the insurance element in working-age benefits is now so minimal and pension entitlement, although based on years of contribution, can be substituted for by means tested social assistance. However, in most other European countries and the US social insurance remains much more important, especially for old age pension entitlement. UK social insurance, national insurance (NI), is a regressive tax in that the threshold for payments is below that for income tax and above an earned income level the rate falls dramatically. Successive Chancellors, most recently Gordon Brown, have regarded NI as a 'hidden tax' – because any changes to it attract much less public and media attention than changes to ordinary income tax – and have used changes to it to increase the overall tax take. In the UK, NI should be consolidated with income tax, made explicitly progressive by reducing the rates of the consolidated tax for lower incomes and applying higher rates of the consolidated tax to higher incomes, and applying the consolidated tax to all incomes rather than as present where NI is only charged on earned incomes. The main political issue here is that the consolidated tax would up the tax burden of higher income pensioners to which the only proper reply is – so what? The rates could easily enough be calibrated so that low income pensioners would pay less and middle income pensioners would see no change in tax charged. Retirement pensions should cease to be based on contribution record and instead become a form of citizen's income on the lines of child benefit. They would be a component of taxable income and therefore there would be a clawback element for high income pensioners. Another important way to make the consolidated tax more progressive would be to allow any tax-exempt income – for example contributions to a pension scheme – to only be exempt at the standard rate of income tax rather than at higher marginal rates. There is a precedent for this in the treatment of tax relief on mortgage income in a period before this was abolished.

It is possible to address the implications for inequality of the introduction of separate taxation for couples in the UK. This is a major source of household inequality and, given the role of high joint household incomes in funding private secondary education, of driving inequality forward down the generations. In the USA, the concept of the household as the fundamental unit to which income taxation is applied is to all intents and purposes retained. In the UK, the domestic arrangements of benefit recipients, including that large majority of working age benefit recipients who are in households where at least one person is in work, are policed quite tightly. It seems only reasonable to apply the same principle to the taxation of income in general. Certainly, serious consideration should be given to taxing couples, although not other residents, based on common real residence in relation to place of work. This would allow for a raising of the point of onset of higher rates of consolidated (NI and income tax) income taxation. Currently in the UK we have the nonsense of a household containing any one individual with an income in excess of £50,000 losing the value of child benefit whereas a household containing a couple each with an income of £49,999 does not! There is real need for a realignment of income taxation of households which would have beneficial effects for overall revenue and would make some tax dodging, for example, appointing a partner as a director of a company set up to receive income instead of that income being taxed directly as income tax, much less advantageous.

Taxation of general wealth, as opposed to wealth in the form of real property and taxation of income derived from wealth, can only really be done when that wealth is transferred from one wealth holder to another on inheritance or in the form of gifts. Inheritance tax alone will not do because holders of wealth will and do transfer it, usually of course to children or other family members, at points which avoid inheritance tax. The tax due should be paid by the recipient of any major wealth transfer at their own marginal rate of the new consolidated income tax. This transfer tax would require reinforcement by a sustained legislative assault on such egregious tax dodges as discretionary trusts. What is required here is a case of back to the future, that is a return to the wealth taxation principles which informed Lloyd George's People's Budget of 1909 and which draw on the same popular discontent which allowed him to make such a radical move. If income is unevenly distributed in post-industrial capitalism, then wealth is much more unevenly distributed. This is a class issue and requires class action.

Taxation of real property is much easier than taxation of any other form of wealth and is already done in most countries through some form of rating based on the value of the real property entity, ownership of which leads to liability to pay the tax. There is much to be said for making the basis of that valuation the land value, although proponents of that approach should read Marx's treatment of rent in *Theories of Surplus Value* which is rather more sophisticated than the simpler approach from Ricardo by way of Henry George which informs the principles they advocate.[5] There is also a useful tax on the transfer of real property in the form of Stamp Duty. The key change here would be to make taxation of real property progressive. Currently it reflects the relative value of the property, although council tax in the UK, despite some useful moves by the Welsh and Scottish governments, is capped in a way which it makes it particularly regressive. We suggest not just removing the cap but making charges at differential progressive rates on bands of the value in the property on the same basis as a progressive income tax.

Of course, if taxes are raised then people will attempt to avoid them. We regard conventional models of the likelihood of avoidance, for example those produced by the UK Institute for Fiscal Studies (IFS), as useless because they take no account of the behavioural modification which would follow on changes in the penalties for avoidance. To impose such penalties would require the introduction of a general anti-avoidance principle into tax legislation which goes far beyond the explicitly 'narrowly defined' rule recently developed in the UK.[6] Richard Murphy of Tax Justice Network is deeply critical of this very narrow and ineffective approach (Murphy, 2012) and we agree with him. What is required is legislation thus as Murphy (2009) proposed and was submitted as an amendment to the Finance Bill 2009 by Pugh and Meacher:

1 If when determining the liability of a person to taxation, duty or similar charge due under statute in the UK it shall be established that a step or steps have been included in a transaction giving rise to that liability or to any claim for an allowance, deduction or relief, with such steps having been included for the sole or one of the main purposes of securing a reduction in that liability to taxation, duty or similar charge with no other material economic purpose for the inclusion of such a step being capable of demonstration by the taxpayer, then subject to the sole exception that the step or steps in question are specifically permitted under the term of any legislation promoted for the specific purpose of permitting

    such use, such step or steps shall be ignored when calculating
    the resulting liability to taxation, duty or similar charge.

2 In the interpretation of this provision a construction that
    would promote the purpose or object underlying the
    provision shall be preferred to a construction that would not
    promote that purpose or object.

That would do the trick in terms of establishing the law. We would go further and consider that the very devising of a scheme to avoid taxation which fell foul of this definition should itself be treated as a criminal offence and subject to penalties. Note that word – 'criminal'. If tax avoidance is to be dealt with then there must be severe penalties and those found to engage in it must be punished harshly. We jail poor people who defraud the benefits system. We should jail rich people who defraud the tax system and we should set the definition of defrauding widely and jail not just those who benefit directly, but also those who engage in what we would treat as a criminal conspiracy with them to that end, the tax advisors in the tax avoidance industry.

Penalties are only half the story. Penalties only work if they are applied and that means the law must be enforced. That means that the tax collection agency must be adequately staffed by public servants committed to the taxation principle and directed by those committed to that principle. We would immediately clear out of the HMRC Board and Senior Management anyone with a history of engagement with tax avoidance, staff it with career tax inspectors appointed with the expectation that their lifetime career will be tax collection with severe financial penalties imposed on them if they take the expertise in which they have been trained at the public expense into the tax avoidance sector. In principle, it would make sense to staff up HMRC and similar agencies right to the point where the on costs of the next member of staff employed were just greater than the tax revenue they would raise if employed. There are few things more nonsensical than cutting the numbers of staff who collect taxes in a time of fiscal crisis.

The last issue to consider is who or what should be liable for taxes. For real property this is relatively easy. The property is within the territory of a state and owes taxes to that state. For consumption taxes this is also easy. For example, for VAT, the transaction takes place within the territory of the state and the tax is owed to that state. Corporation tax would be handled by the principle of country by country accounting. For personal income and wealth taxes we suggest following the principle adopted by the United States. If you are a US citizen or even resident non-citizen then you are liable for US taxes wherever you live. There are provisions which allow the avoidance of double taxation but the general principle should hold. If you have the passport then you pay the tax. All the vile dodges of the non-dom resident in the UK, living at the weekend in Monaco and working during the week in the City of London, and so on, would be dealt with either by this principle or extended legislation to the same effect. We would argue that Monaco, Lichenstein and similar pest holes should be expelled from the global community of nations and denied recognition as legitimate states. Their taxation policies amount to economic warfare against welfare capitalism. They are rogue states and should be treated as such. In the UK, the special status of the City of London as a governance entity should be abolished. The UK is in serious risk of having rogue status itself in relation to tax avoidance and in a right-dominated post-Brexit condition this would be a serious possibility.

Can it be done?

Parties of the centre-left in the countries which adopted welfare capitalism have largely abandoned one of their most important historic functions – the education of the populations as to the reality of exploitation and the need to elect to power political parties prepared to do something about it, both by reinforcing the ability of trade unions to act effectively and by using taxation and spending on welfare broadly defined to redistribute from exploiters to exploited. This is not a matter of ideological imposition. David Byrne remembers that nearly 60 years ago in his first Latin lesson he was taught that 'educate' comes from the Latin *educare* – to draw out from, not put into. The complex systems of welfare capitalism are in a state of crisis. If we return to one of the most important things E.P. Thompson ever wrote, his definition of the distinction between Experience I and Experience II, then that helps us in understanding the possibilities here. Thompson (1981) defined 'Experience II' as the understanding of the social order created by all the pressures brought to bear on people's mindsets by the pressures of the media and what we might call the ideological state apparatuses – what 'they' tell us things are like. 'Experience I' is our understandings as shaped by lived experience in relation to the character of the capitalist social order. Key aspects of this lived experience are of course exploitation and crisis. As Thompson puts it, the impact of Experience I on our understanding and behaviour 'cannot be infinitely postponed, falsified or suppressed by ideology'. In a lovely phrase he asserts: 'it walks in the door without knocking'. In the aftermath of the crisis and with the imposition of austerity Experience I is through the door and half way up the stairs.

> Experience I is in eternal friction with imposed consciousness, and, as it breaks through, we, who fight in all the intricate vocabularies and disciplines of Experience II, are given moments of openness and opportunity before the mould of ideology is imposed once more. (Thompson, 1981, 406)

People are living with crisis in all its aspects. Those who benefited from the good years of industrial welfare capitalism are both under attack themselves and for the first time in nearly 200 years are a generation whose children will be poorer than they are themselves.

The USA is in a very bad state. Trump is no real populist. All the signs from his transition appointments and proposals in relation to taxation and welfare is that this man elected by those who have lost the gains of industrial welfare capitalism is about to reward the rich, remove banking regulations imposed after the crash, further erode the organisational rights of workers, and destroy crucial elements of welfare gains in social security and healthcare. By comparison Nicola

Sturgeon's SNP looks like the Left Opposition in the Bolsheviks in the 1920s. Things are not quite so bad in Europe.

This is a moment of openness and opportunity and it will be the pity of the world if the left do not take it. They need to educate in the sense of providing a vocabulary and grammar which makes sense of the situation people are in and offering a framework of policy which shows that another world is possible – the old promise of democratic socialism. Complex systems have multiple but not infinite futures within the possibility space. In complex social systems it is human action which determines which of those futures will come to pass. Radical reform of taxation, made possible by a political programme which has stirred up as much class antagonism about the unfairness and exploitative character of taxation in post-industrial financialised capitalism as possible, is one of the mechanisms which can be brought into play in the drive towards a restoration of greater equality, of acceptable levels of inequality, in the future. It will not be enough on its own. We need a reassertion of the role of planning in the general economy, the crucial meso element in economic management, with an emphasis on genuine production of things – including such immaterial things as decent elderly care – as opposed to speculation in property and money.

In some places this will be easier than others. In 1990 the UK generated 17 per cent of its value added from manufacturing and 5.5 per cent from finance and insurance. The figures for Sweden were 21 per cent from manufacturing and 6.3 per cent from finance and insurance. In 2015 the UK generated 9.8 per cent of value added from manufacturing and 7.2 per cent from finance and insurance. Sweden generated 17 per cent from manufacturing and 4.6 per cent from finance and insurance.[7] It will be a lot easier for Sweden to manage its transition to post-industrial welfare capitalism than it will be for the UK, but we have to try.

Notes

[1] The role of discretionary trusts as a means of avoiding estate duty has been crucial in subverting the attempts to break up great inherited wealth which began in the UK with Lloyd George's 'People's Budget' of 1909 which was intended exactly to fund the Liberal Welfare Reforms, the foundation for the subsequent Welfare State of UK industrial capitalism.

[2] The rather more robust than HMRC US Internal Revenue Service prosecuted Helmsley and she was sentenced to 13 years in jail – that's the way to do it.

[3] See www.appgresponsibletax.org.uk/tax-justice-network/

[4] The term real property – real estate – refers to any property which incorporates land and improvements to that land.

[5] Basically, Marx allows for improvements to land to become incorporated in the land as opposed to standing separate from it. Given that, for example, domestic property is to all intents and purposes immortal and therefore no depreciation can be charged on it for tax allowance purposes, this principle is already incorporated in real property valuation.

[6] For a useful discussion of these issues see Seely (2016), although this is deeply conservative in its consideration of the role of tax avoidance legislation.

[7] The pesthole of Luxemburg generates nearly 25 per cent of its GVA from the finance sector – another rogue state to be dealt with as firmly as possible.

References

Aalbers, M.B. (2016) *The Financialization of Housing*, ebook, London: Routledge

Adam, S., Besley, T., Blundell, R. et al (2010) *Dimensions of Tax Design*, Oxford: Oxford University Press

Adam, S., Johnson, P. and Roantree, B. (2013) Taxing and independent Scotland, *Institute of Fiscal Studies (IFS) Briefing Note* BN141, London: IFS

Alt, J., Preston, I. and Sibieta, L. (2010) The political economy of tax policy, in J. Mirrlees (ed) *Dimensions of Tax Design*, Chapter 14 (pp 1204–315), Oxford: Oxford University Press (for Institute of Fiscal Studies)

APPG (All Party Parliamentary Group) on Responsible Tax (2016) *A More Responsible Global Tax System or a 'Sticking Plaster'?*, London: APPG Responsible Tax, www.appgresponsibletax.org.uk/wp-content/uploads/2016/08/Sticking-Plaster-APPG-Responsible-Tax-Report.pdf

Alvaredo, F., Atkinson, A., Piketty, T. and Saez, E. (2013) The top 1 percent in international and historical perspective, *Journal of Economic Perspectives* 27, 3, 3–20

Alvaredo, F., Atkinson, A. and Morelli, S. (2016) The challenge of measuring UK wealth inequality in the 2000s, *Fiscal Studies* 37, 1, 13–33

Amior, M., Crawford, R. and Tetlow, G. (2013) *The Fiscal Sustainability of an Independent Scotland*, London: Institute of Fiscal Studies

Andreski, S. (1954) *Military Organization and Society*, London: Routledge and Kegan Paul

Anyaegbu, G. (2011) The effects of taxes and benefits on income inequality,1980–2009/10, *Economic and Labour Market Review* 5, I, 53–72

Atkinson, A. and Leigh, A. (2010) *The distribution of top incomes in five Anglo-Saxon countries over the twentieth century*, Discussion Paper No. 640, Australian National University Centre for Economic Policy Research

Bailey, J., Coward, J. and Whittaker, M. (2011) *Painful Separation: An International Study of the Weakening Relationship Between Wage Growth and the Pay of Ordinary Workers*, London: Resolution Foundation

Beatty, C. and Fothergill, S. (2016) *The Uneven Impact of Welfare Reform*, Sheffield: Centre for Regional Economic and Social Research, Sheffield Hallam University

Belfield, C., Cribb, J., Hood, A. and Joyce, R. (2016) *Living Standards, Poverty and Inequality in the UK: 2016*, London: Institute for Fiscal Studies

Bell, B. and Van Reenen, J. (2010) *Bankers' Pay and Extreme Wage Inequality in the UK*, London: Centre for Economic Policy Research (CEPR), London School of Economics and Political Science (LSE)

Berthier, A. (2014) The Scottish rate of income tax and additional rate taxpayers, *Scottish Parliament Information Centre (SPICe) Financial Scrutiny Unit Briefing*, Edinburgh: The Scottish Parliament

Beveridge, W. (1944) *Full Employment in a Free Society*, London: Allen and Unwin

BIS (Department for Business, Innovation and Skills) (2016) *Trade Union Membership 2015: Statistical Bulletin*, London: BIS

Blair, A. and Schroeder, G. (1999) *Europe: The Third Way*, Bonn: Friedrich Ebert Foundation

Block, F. (1981) The fiscal crisis of the state, *Annual Review of Sociology* 7, 1–27

Blyth, M. (2013a) *Austerity: The History of a Dangerous Idea*, Oxford: Oxford University Press

Blyth, M. (2013b) Austerity as ideology: A reply to my critics, *Comparative European Politics* 11, 6, 737–51

Bonica, A., McCarty, N., Poole, K.T. and Rosenthal, H. (2013) Why hasn't democracy slowed rising economic inequality?, *Journal of Economic Perspectives* 27, 3, 103–24

Burkhauser, R.V., Hérault, N., Jenkins, S.P. and Wilkins, R. (2016) *What has been happening to UK income inequality since the mid-1990s? Answers from reconciled and combined household survey and tax return data*, Discussion Paper no. 9718, Bonn: Institute for the Study of Labor (IZA)

Byrne, D.S. (1998) *Complexity theory and the social sciences: An introduction*, London: Routledge

Byrne, D.S. (2005) *Social exclusion*, Maidenhead: Open University Press

Byrne, D.S. and Callaghan, G. (2013) *Complexity Theory and the Social Sciences: The State of the Art*, London: Routledge

Campbell, A. (2016) *Scottish Government Proposals for Council Tax Reform*, Edinburgh: Scottish Parliament Information Centre (SPICe) Castells, M. (1996) *The Rise of the Network Society*, Oxford: Blackwell

Chandler, M. (2016) *Contracts that do not Guarantee a Minimum Number of Hours*, London: Office of National Statistics, www.ons.gov.uk/employmentandlabourmarket/peopleinwork/earningsandworkinghours/articles/contractsthatdonotguaranteeaminimumnumberofhours/september2016

City of London Corporation (2015) *Total Tax Contribution of UK Financial Services 8th Edition*, London: City of London Corporation

Collinson, P. (2015) One in 65 UK adults now a millionaire, figures show, *Guardian* 27 August

Corlett, A., Finch, D. and Whittaker, M. (2016) *Living Standards 2016 The Experiences of Low to Middle Income Households in Downturn and Recovery*, London: Resolution Foundation

Comparative European Politics (2013) Symposium on Blyth, *Comparative European Politics* 11, 6, 705–12 Crouch, C. (2000) *Coping with Post-Democracy*, London: Fabian Society

Crouch, C. (2011) *The Strange Non-Death of Neo-Liberalism*, Cambridge: Polity

DBIS (Department for Business, Innovation and Skills) (2016) *Trade Union Membership 2015: Statistical Bulletin*, London: DBIS

Dorling, D. (2015) *Inequality and the 1%*, London: Verso

Experian (2010) *Seasonal Sense*, www.experian.co.uk/assets/background-checking/white-papers/seasonal-sense-temporary-recruitment-whitepaper.pdf

Farnsworth, K. (2015) *The British Corporate Welfare State: Public Provision for Private Business*, Sheffield: Sheffield Political Economy Research Institute, University of Sheffield

Farnsworth, K. and Irving, Z. (2011) *Social Policy in Challenging Times*, Bristol: Policy Press

Farnsworth, K. and Irving, Z. (eds) (2015) *Social Policy in Times of Austerity*, Bristol: Policy Press

Feagin, J. (1987) The secondary circuit of capital, *International Journal of Urban and Regional Research* 11, 2, 172–92

Giddens, A. (1998) *The Third Way: The Renewal of Social Democracy*, Cambridge: Polity

Glynn, A. and Sutcliffe, B. (1972) *British Workers and the Profits Squeeze*, Harmondsworth: Penguin

Harvey, D. (1999) *The Limits to Capital*, Oxford: Blackwell

High Pay Centre (2016) *The State of Pay: Briefing on Executive Pay*, London: High Pay Centre

HMRC (Her Majesty's Revenue and Customs) (2016a) *Personal Income Statistics 2014*, London: HMRC

HMRC (Her Majesty's Revenue and Customs) (2016b) *Corporation Tax Statistics*, London: HMRC

Hobsbawm, E. (1995) The golden years, in *The Age of Extremes: The Short Twentieth Century, 1914–1991*, pp. 257–86 (Chapter 9), London: Abacus

Hobsbawm, E. and Rudé, G. (1969) *Captain Swing*, London: Verso (2014)

Horton, T. and Reed, H. (2010) *Where the Money Goes: How we Benefit from Public Services*, London: Trades Union Congress (TUC)

Houlder, V. (2016) Budget 2016: A stealthy revolution in UK tax system, *Financial Times*, March 16

House of Commons Work and Pensions Committee (2014) *Fraud and error in the benefits system*, London: House of Commons, www.publications.parliament.uk/pa/cm201314/cmselect/cmworpen/1082/108205.htm

House of Lords Select Committee on Economic Affairs (2013) *The Economic Implications for the United Kingdom of Scottish Independence*, 2nd Report of Session 2012–13, London: House of Lords

ILO (International Labour Organisation) (2015) Labour relations and collective bargaining, *Issue Brief* 1, London: ILO

Johnson, P. and Sibieta, L. (2011) *Top Income Growth Drives Rise in Income Inequality under Labour*, London: Institute for Fiscal Studies

Johnson, P. and Phillips, D. (2012) *Scottish Independence: The Fiscal Context*, Institute of Fiscal Studies (IFS) BN135, London: IFS

JRF (Joseph Rowntree Foundation) (2016) *Monitoring Poverty and Social Exclusion 2016*, York: JRF

Kung, H. (1997) *A Global Ethic for Global Politics and Economics*, London: SCM Press

Lansley, S. (2011) *The Cost of Inequality: Why Economic Equality is Essential for Recovery*, London: Gibson Square

Lansley, S. (2016) The loaded dice: Pro rich state policy is bad news for the poor and the economy, *Radical Statistics* 115, 23–36

Lansley, S. and Reed, H. (2013) *How to Boost the Wage Share*, London: Trades Union Congress (TUC)Lefebvre, H. (1991) *The Production of Space*, Oxford: Blackwell

MacInnes, T., Tinson, A., Hughes, C., Barry Born, T. and Aldridge, H. (2015) *Monitoring Poverty and Social Exclusion 2015*, York: Joseph Rowntree Foundation

Massey, D., Dorling, D. and Murphy, R. (2015) *The Greatest Invention: Tax and the Campaign for a Just Society*, London: Commonwealth

Meyer, H. (2016) Reviving the promise of prosperity in the European Union, *IMK Research Essay* 10, Dussledorf: IMK Macroeconomic Policy Institute, Hans Böckler Stiftung, www.socialeurope.eu/wp-content/uploads/2016/12/RE10-Meyer.pdf

Miller, H. and Pope, T. (2016) *The Changing Composition of UK Tax Revenues*, London: Institute for Fiscal Studies

Mirrlees, J., Adam, S., Besley, T. et al (2011) *Tax by Design: The Mirrlees Review*, Oxford: Oxford University Press

Mishel L., Bivens, J., Gould, E. and Shierholz, H. (2012) *The State of Working America*, 12th edn, Ithaca, NY: Cornell University Press (for Economic Policy Institute)

Murphy, R. (2009) What would a general anti-avoidance provision look like? *Tax Research UK Blog*, www.taxresearch.org.uk/Blog/2009/05/06/what-would-a-general-anti-avoidance-provision-look-like/

Murphy, R. (2012) Why we need a genuine general anti-avoidance principle to beat tax abuse, *Tax Research UK Blog*, www.taxresearch.org.uk/Blog/2012/06/20/why-we-need-a-genuine-general-anti-avoidance-principle-to-beat-tax-abuse-2/

Murphy, R. (2014) *The Tax Gap*, London: Press Computer Systems (PCS), www.taxresearch.org.uk/Blog/2014/09/22/new-report-the-tax-gap-is-119-4-billion-and-rising/

Murphy, R. and Christensen, J. (2013) *Tax Us If You Can*, 2nd edn, London: Tax Justice Network, www.taxresearch.org.uk/Blog/2013/02/01/tax-us-if-you-can-second-edition/

NAO (National Audit Office) (2012) *Tax avoidance: tackling marketed avoidance schemes*, London: NAO

Nelson, J.I. (1995) *Post-Industrial Capitalism*, London: Sage

O'Connor, J. (1973) *The Fiscal Crisis of the State*, New York: Saint Martin's Press

O'Connor, J. (2002) *The Fiscal Crisis of the State* (with a new introduction by the author), New Brunswick, NJ: Transaction Publishers (2009)

OECD (Organization for Economic Cooperation and Development) (no date) *Details of Tax Revenue UK*, https://stats.oecd.org/Index.aspx?DataSetCode=REVGBR

OECD (Organization for Economic Cooperation and Development) (2013), *Action Plan on Base Erosion and Profit Shifting*, Paris: OECD Publishing

OECD (Organization for Economic Cooperation and Development) (2016) *Productivity Statistics*, www.oecd-ilibrary.org/employment/data/oecd-productivity-statistics_pdtvy-data-en

ONS (Office for National Statistics) (2016a) *The Effects of Taxes and Benefits on Household Income, Historical Datasets*, Newport: ONS

ONS (Office for National Statistics) (2016b) *The Effects of Taxes and Benefits on Household Income, Methodology and Coherence: Financial Year Ending 2015*, Newport: ONS

ONS (Office for National Statistics) (2016c) *The Effects of Taxes and Benefits on Income Inequality: 1977 to Financial Year Ending 2015*, Newport: ONS

ONS (Office for National Statistics) (2016d) *Effects of Taxes and Benefits on Household Income: Financial Year Ending 2015*, Newport: ONS

Phillips, D. (2014) Business as usual: The Barnett Formula, business rates and further tax devolution, *Institute of Fiscal Studies (IFS) Briefing Note* BN155, London: IFS

Phillips, D. and Tetlow, G. (2014) Taxation, government spending and the public finances of Scotland: Updating the medium-term outlook, *Institute of Fiscal Studies (IFS) Briefing Note* BN148, London: IFS

Pizzigati, S. (2012) *The Rich Don't Always Win*, New York: Seven Stories Press

Polanyi, K. (1944) *The Great Transformation*, Boston, MA: Beacon Press (2001)

Pope, T. and Waters, T. (2016) *A Survey of the UK Tax System*, London: Institute for Fiscal Studies Briefing Note BN09

Reed, H. and Mohun Himmelweit, J. (2012) *Where Have All the Wages Gone?*, London: Trades Union Congress (TUC)Robinson, J. (1962) *Economic Philosophy*, London: C.A. Watts

Ruiz, N. and Woloszko, N. (2015) What do household surveys suggest about the top 1% incomes and inequality in OECD countries?, *Organization for Economic Cooperation and Development (OECD) Economics Department Working Paper* 1265, Paris: OECD Publishing, http://dx.doi.org/10.1787/5jrs556f36zt-en

Sayer, A. (2016) *Why We Can't Afford the Rich*, Bristol: Policy Press

Schumpeter, J.A. (1918) *The Crisis of the Tax State*, Graz, Leipzig: Leuschner and Lubensky.

Scottish Government (2016) *The Impact of an Increase in the Additional Rate of income tax from 45p to 50p in Scotland*, Edinburgh: Scottish Government

Seely, A. (2016) Tax avoidance: A general anti-abuse rule, *House of Commons Briefing Paper* 06265, London: House of Commons

Shaxson, N. and Christensen, J. (2013) *The Finance Curse: How Oversized Financial Centres Attack Democracy and Corrupt Economies*, London: Tax Justice Network, www.taxjustice.net/cms/upload/pdf/Finance_Curse_Final.pdf

Sikka, P. (2015) The hand of accounting and accountancy firms in deepening income and wealth inequalities and the economic crisis: Some evidence, *Critical Perspectives on Accounting* 30, 46–62

Sinfield, A. (2016) How much austerity is there in tax welfare?, *Paper* given at the Social Policy Association annual conference, Belfast

Skocpol, T. (1995) *Social Policy in the United States: Future Possibilities in Historical Perspective*, Princeton, NJ: Princeton University Press

Standing, G. (2011) *The Precariat: The New Dangerous Class*, London: Bloomsbury

Streeck, W. (2013a) The politics of public debt: Neoliberalism, capitalist development, and the restructuring of the state, *Max Planck Institute for the Study of Society (MPIfG) Discussion Paper* 13/7, Cologne: MPIfG

Streeck, W. (2013b) Will expansion work? On Mark Blyth, *Austerity: The history of a dangerous idea*, *Comparative European Politics* 11, 6, 722–28

Thompson, E.P. (1981) The politics of theory, in R. Samuel (ed) *Peoples' History and Socialist Theory*, pp. 396–408, London: Routledge and Kegan Paul

Titmuss, R. (1958) *Essays on the Welfare State*, London: George Allen and Unwin

Titmuss, R. (1965) *Income Distribution and Social Change*, London: George Allen and Unwin

Tonkin, R. (2015) *The Effects of Taxes and Benefits on Household Income, Financial Year Ending 2014: Methodology and Coherence*, Newport: ONS (Office for National Statistics)

Unger, R. (2014) Where has the Social Democratic left gone wrong?, Speech at the *Royal Society of Arts* 2014, www.socialeurope. eu/2014/01/social-democratic-left/

Unger, R. and Wood, S. (2014) Juncture interview: Roberto Unger on the means and ends of the political left, *IPPR*, 22 January, www.ippr.org/juncture/juncture-interview-roberto-unger-on-the-means-and-ends-of-the-political-left

Westergaard, J. (1978) Social policy and class inequality: Some notes on welfare state limits, in R. Milliband and J. Saville (eds) *The Socialist Register 1978*, pp. 71–99, London: Merlin Press

Whitfield, D. (2016) *The Financial Commodification of Public Infrastructure*, European Services Strategy Unit Research Report 8, www. european-services-strategy.org.uk/publications/essu-research-reports/the-financial-commodification-of-public-infras/financial-commodification-public-infrastructure.pdf

WID (Wealth and Income Database) (2016) Wealth and Income Database, http://wid.world/world/#sfiinc_p99p100_z/US;FR;DE;CN;ZA;GB/last/eu/k/p/yearly/s/false/4.725/30/curve/false

Williams, R. (1958) *Culture and Society*, London: Chatto and Windus

Williams, R. (1980) Base and superstructure in Marxist cultural theory, in *Problems in Materialism and Culture: Selected Essays*, pp. 31–49, London: Verso and New Left Books (NLB)

Index

Page numbers in bold refer to a table or figure in the text.

Scott Commission 109
Scottish Independence
  Referendum 11, 105, 107–8
Scottish Labour 105, 106, 108
Scottish Nationalist Party (SNP)
  11, 105, 106, 107, 110–11,
  131
Scottish NHS 106
self-employment 21–2, 34–5,
  41–2, 44, 92
service industry **118**
shareholder movement 88
Shaxon, N. and Christensen,
  J. 50
Sinfield, A. 47
single-family households 35, 46
Skocpol, T. 39
social assistance 5, 35, 36, 124
social care 24, 27–8, 61, 63–4
social class 25, 113
  elite class 9, 66, 105
  working classes 4–5, 6, 64–6,
  80, 87, 105–6, 119
social complexity theory 2
Social Democratic Party 10, 57,
  64–5, 66, 101–2, 119
  Germany 3, 58, 101–2
social insurance 8, 33, 34–5,
  41–2, 62, 64, 102, 113, 124–5
  Germany 3–4, 39, 41, 58
  and industrial capitalism 3–4,
  5, 12n5, 39–42
  and pensions 39, 63
  US 39–40, 41, 42, 113, 124
  see also national insurance
socialism 4–5, 20, 64–5, 66,
  101–2, 104, 116n13, 119, 131
  Germany 17–18, 58
social order 3–4, 7, 8, 9, 11,
  19–20, 119, 130
social reform 3, 4, 18, 39,
  101–2
social security 34, 36, 45, 113

social systems 2, 131
Solidarity Taxes 44–5
Southern Cross 27–8
Spain 94
speculation 53, 55–6, 88
Speenhamland supplements 6,
  37–9, 51n7
Stalinism 114
Stamp Duty 29, 127
standards of care 63
Standing, G. 24
state sector *see* public/state
  sector
Streeck, W. 9, 55, 58–60, 61,
  67, 108
Sturgeon, Nicola 108
surplus, social 20
surplus value 17, 19, 55–6, 62
Sweden **91**, 131
sweetheart deals 48, 122
Swing riots 38
Swiss bank accounts 47, 122
Switzerland 94

T

taxation, direct 70, 71–4, **75**,
  80
taxation, indirect
  and inequality 70, 74–8, 80,
  97, 98
  as regressive taxation 30, 74,
  76, 77
  and tax revenue 17, 29, 30,
  90, 97, 98
taxation, personal 10, 70–99
taxation, regressive 30, 42, 47,
  82–3
  and council tax 73, 80, 110,
  127
  and indirect taxation 30, 74,
  76, 77
  and national insurance 109,
  124